Betting It All

The Entrepreneurs of Technology

M I C H A E L   S.   M A L O N E

JOHN WILEY & SONS, INC.

To anyone who has ever bet it all.

Copyright © 2002 by Michael S. Malone. All rights reserved.

Published by John Wiley & Sons, Inc., New York.
Published simultaneously in Canada.

This publication is designed to provide accurate and authoritative information in regard to the subject matter covered. It is sold with the understanding that the publisher is not engaged in rendering professional services. If professional advice or other expert assistance is required, the services of a competent professional person should be sought.

Library of Congress Cataloging-in-Publication Data:

Malone, Michael S. (Michael Shawn), 1954-
    Betting it all: the entrepreneurs of technology/Michael S. Malone.
        p. cm.
    Includes bibliographical references and index.
    ISBN 0-471-20190-1 (cloth: alk. paper)
    1. Businesspeople—United States—Biography.   2. Businesspeople—United States—Interviews.   3. Computer industry—United States—Biography   4. Computer software industry—United States—Biography   5. Microelectronics industry—United States—Biography   6. Entrepreneurship—United States—Case studies.   7. Microelectronics industry—California—Santa Clara County—History.   8. Santa Clara County (Calif.)—Biography.   9. Risk.   I. Title.
    HC102.5.A2M32   2001
    338.4'7004'092273—dc21
    [B]   2001045447

Printed in the United States of America.

10 9 8 7 6 5 4 3 2 1

CONTENTS

ACKNOWLEDGMENTS

If there is one thing that we have learned in the last year it is that multimedia projects require the combined efforts of a small array of talented and dedicated people.

Before *Betting It All: The Entrepreneurs of Technology* was a book, it was a television series. And that series would have stayed on the drawing board had we not received the backing of our main underwriter, Applied Materials Corporation, and, in particular, Chairman and CEO James Morgan and Tom Hayes, Managing Director of Global Corporate Affairs. For a dozen years, they have always been there to support our work. We are also grateful for the additional underwriting from the Mayfield Fund, Hewlett-Packard Co., and Goldman Sachs. That support carried us down the homestretch.

By the same token, our production partners' dedication to the documentary was worth more than gold. We appreciate the support and hard work of Ed Carlstone from Television and Associates and Tom Fanella, Bill Matthews, and Linda Dennis from KTEH—TV. In addition, we couldn't have hoped for better film crews at the two studios.

To complete the book at a fast and furious pace always required the already busy people at *Forbes ASAP* to go beyond the call of duty. We got that and more from Mike Boland, researcher, David de la Fuente, copy editor, Gloria Emelson, proofreader, and Beth Brann, *ASAP*'s production manager.

We are thankful for the support of Tim Forbes and Forbes, Inc., in all of our myriad endeavors. We also wish to single out Laurie Baker and Monie Begley of Forbes' PR Department. The fact that you know about this documentary and book is likely due to their efforts.

Finally, we would like to acknowledge John Wiley & Sons Publishers, Inc., especially our editor, Matt Holt, for supporting this project. And our agent, the legendary Don Congdon, who has, as always, stood in our corner.

Robert Grove, Executive Producer
Michael S. Malone, Host and Author
Ann McAdam, Associate Producer and Editor

FOREWORD

I have spent most of my life among the men and women who build companies and I still find them endlessly interesting.

As the chairman and chief executive officer of the world's largest semiconductor equipment company, a board member of a number of companies and nonprofits, and a longtime resident of Silicon Valley, I suspect that I have run across virtually every major technology entrepreneur inside the Valley—and many of those outside of it.

They are an amazing, diverse group, from newly arrived immigrants to industry veterans. And more and more of them are women. For those of us involved in business, this is only good news—it means a robust and dynamic economy. As a citizen, I take great pride in knowing that the melting pot of America is growing ever more egalitarian. Ambition, courage, and hard work can reward everyone, not just a select few.

Applied Materials is proud to be the lead underwriter for *Betting It All*, and in watching the series I was struck by a number of observations. First, despite the fact that I personally know many of the entrepreneurs—some for years, I gained fascinating new insights and information about these men and women. In these interviews, you hear about the lives of entrepreneurs from their own perspective. You find candid insights and observations about the challenges in their lives and how they applied them to find success.

I guess that is the point—and the triumph—of *Betting It All*. It plumbs the characters of some of the most celebrated people in the world and discovers something stunning and new every time. On the television shows, these moments flash by so fast that it's hard to hold on to them. That is what makes this book so welcome: It is not only a written record of the interviews, but a description of what went on around them—the comments that were cut out of the show, and the behavior of the guests before the lights went on and after the director yelled "cut."

The miracle is how Mike Malone, Bob Grove, and the rest of the *Forbes ASAP* team managed to capture such candid moments from such skilled and experienced interviewees. As a top executive, like these entrepreneurs, I know that every public statement I make will be replayed and reprinted and scrutinized for clues to my own leadership style and the financial health of my company. Needless to say, that kind of scrutiny tends to make you circumspect pretty fast. When you know that the livelihoods of thousands of people rest on your words, you tend to measure those words very carefully.

On the other hand, I also have been interviewed several times by Mike Malone, and I know how effective an interrogator he can be. After all, he grew up and worked in Silicon Valley, so he is like a trusted member of the family. It seems that he has always been there. I remember that he was a young cub reporter sitting in the audience at some of my earliest speeches as Applied Materials CEO in the 1970s. With Mike, the conversation comes so easily that you can forget that he is a celebrated journalist—right up to the moment he asks you that penetrating and personal question. Suddenly it is too late to go silent, and you say things you may have bottled up for years.

Watching the series, and now again reading the interviews, I find myself wincing when Malone asks the under-the-skin question. Publicists watching from the control room must have felt faint. And yet, there is a lesson here as well: To my mind, each of the guests comes to life, appearing more noble, more decent, and ultimately more human than they ever do in other interview settings. These are the real entrepreneurial titans I know—the complicated, smart, and sensitive people I work with when the cameras and the notebooks aren't around.

Thanks to *Betting It All*, now you get to meet them, too.

Jim Morgan, CEO
Applied Materials

INTRODUCTION

I once understood entrepreneurs.

Having grown up in Silicon Valley, I spent much of my childhood with many of the men (and boys) who would one day create the electronics revolution. As a young newspaper reporter, I spent my days interviewing and writing about the founders of the latest hot tech companies. On several occasions, bitten by the bug, I became an entrepreneur myself. I spent two years at one ill-starred start-up, never saw a dime, and starved. I spent a few weeks with another and made more money than I would have in a lifetime of work.

After all of these experiences, I fancied myself an expert on new companies and the people who founded them. It was a good time to have such expertise: High-tech entrepreneurs, in Silicon Valley and other electronics enclaves, were transforming society, driving the economy to new heights. They were the heroes of the age. For my part, I wrote books on entrepreneurship, was quoted regularly by my fellow reporters, and, when asked, would pontificate endlessly on the subject.

In my mind, an entrepreneur was an extraordinarily complex creature, identified by numerous distinct traits. When I wrote about such a person, I had in my mind's eye a 40-year-old man of European (occasionally Asian) lineage, probably raised in the Midwest, with a graduate degree in engineering or physics, and a prickly—even aggressive—personality. In other words, the very image of that generation of extraordinary men who came of age in the 1950s and founded the semiconductor industry.

I would say knowingly, "Did you know that researchers have found that entrepreneurs have a personality most like—not corporate CEOs or even (chuckle) Mafia torpedoes—but Peace Corps volunteers?" I would then usually add that most entrepreneurs are so difficult and antisocial that they can't do anything else.

I couldn't have been more wrong. I was like a scientist stuck with a theory that no longer quite worked. Somehow I managed to shoehorn into this ideological straitjacket personalities as diverse as the saintly Gordon Moore of Intel, the volcanic Charlie Sporck of National Semiconductor, the flamboyant Jerry Sanders, and the godlike David Packard.

The disconnect grew even greater as subsequent waves of new entrepreneurs rode onto the scene. Some were neighbors, like the childlike Steve Wozniak and the charismatic and dangerous Steve Jobs. Some were aging hippies; others were proto-nerds like Bill Gates. Others were so far out of the normal flow of life as to be not antisocial but simply asocial. How did they fit my template?

They were followed by buttoned-down corporate types who built equally sober companies in workstations and computer-aided design. Then came immigrants, from India, Vietnam, China, and almost everywhere. Then hustlers, slick salesmen, ex-jocks. Then women engineers and smooth corporate types. And then, in the late 1990s with the rise of the Internet, *everybody* became an entrepreneur.

Or at least it seemed that way. For a span of 24 months, I found myself interviewing, or hearing presentations from, or investing in, ambitious senior citizens, postadolescents with nose rings, ex-cops, fine arts majors, other reporters, buttoned-down corporate types, former CEOs of giant companies, and housewives—all of them self-proclaimed entrepreneurs, with business plans under their arms (and sometimes enormous venture capital checks in their pockets), ready to conquer the world. In the face of such an onslaught I finally had to abandon my comfortable stereotype about entrepreneurs. And it was during this period of confusion that Bob Grove and I devised *Betting It All*.

The idea for the television series arose, as have most of our good ideas, from a conversation over lunch in a local bar. CNBC was on the television, announcing yet one more unbelievable day in the stock market. Electronics stocks, especially Internet shares, were reaching nosebleed heights, far above any traditional rule of valuation. It seemed as if the world had turned upside down. Young entrepreneurs, mere children with no previous business experience, were becoming billionaires. Bob and I didn't know whether to cheer or cry.

Instead, we talked. About the entrepreneurs we knew. Young and old. Men and women. Those who had built great companies or suffered great failures. Were the company builders of a generation ago really different from the ones we now saw congratulating themselves on TV? Or were these merely the same old characters in New Age mufti?

What if, Bob and I asked each other, we were to gather the most successful entrepreneurs we knew, aim a camera at them, and ask them, not about their current business strategies, but about themselves? What if we asked them not only about their obvious successes, but also about their most painful failures? And about what their choice of career had cost them?

Perhaps if we did, we might get past the carefully crafted firewall presented by their PR staff and see these men and women as they really are. We might even finally find the right answer to what makes a person become an entrepreneur.

The idea was too compelling to let go, even in the face of putting out a magazine undergoing its own period of explosive growth. Even before we started, we knew the logistics were going to be a nightmare: We would have to bring together a dozen or more of the most powerful (and busy) business executives on earth, having already convinced them to talk about their childhood, their greatest fears, and their biggest failures.

Luckily, Bob and I had a secret weapon: Associate Producer Ann McAdam, half our age and with twice our tenacity. It was Ann who cajoled, wheedled, and pushed the guests to commit to appear at the studio on a specified date—and these tycoons, these Masters of the Digital Universe, almost to a person, agreed.

We had contacted Tom Fanella, general manager of San Jose's PBS affiliate, KTEH-TV, and asked if he wanted to be the host station. We had a long history there: My public television interview program was based there for all of its eight years, and Bob had worked there as executive producer of *Silicon Valley Report*. Tom was enthusiastic, but with one caveat: We would have to move both the set and the shoot somewhere else during pledge periods.

Luckily, we knew of another studio 10 miles north in Mountain View—TVA Inc., where Bob had shot a number of episodes of *Computer Chronicles*. There, Ed Carlstone, TVA's president, not only accepted our proposal but agreed to be a cosponsor.

And so, for a period of three weeks, we became Silicon Valley gypsies, moving from one studio to another. The shoots themselves were marathons. Pressed for time because of the magazine, with limited funds, we scheduled as many as three interviews per day. That's hard enough when interviewing authors and politicians, but the guests on *Betting It All* were some of the most forceful personalities of our time. As a result, after a day of studying notes, changing suits between shoots, and being emotionally pummeled by the guests for hours, I would go home and fall asleep in a chair . . . and be back the next day for more of the same.

The demands on Bob and Ann were even greater. Managing everything from the control room was the ever cool Mr. Grove. Bob not only directed every shot, but also dealt with broken cameras, touchy microphones, and truculent PR flacks—and still managed to come up with a handful of incisive questions for me to ask at the end of each interview. He also edited the series and transcribed all the interviews for this book—all while writing major investigative stories for the magazine on America Online and Internet crime.

Meanwhile, Ann orchestrated the guests' travel right up to the moment they arrived in the studio, then greeted them, distracted the handlers, managed the still photographer, dealt with various emergencies, and 10 minutes later started over with the next guest. For this book, Ann convinced these same guests to temporarily surrender their most cherished personal photographs. She also pulled all of the component parts together, managing the fact checking, editing, releases, and contracts. Bob and I may have devised the television series, but Ann created this book.

In the end, did we succeed? Obviously, that is a judgment each reader must make. As always with such projects, I, myself, am unsure. On the one hand, I think this book is a unique document: No one has ever plumbed the souls of high-tech tycoons so deeply; no book has ever looked so far past the boardroom façade of so many business leaders to find the real people huddled behind. For that, I am especially proud.

Yet, at the same time, as with almost everything I've ever done with television, I am also disappointed. Thirty minutes is such a brief time to tell a person's life story, to capture the nuances of their personal ethos. Too many times, as with Gates, we broke through— only to run out the clock and have the guest whisked off to the next meeting. These are also the most guarded of public figures: Even when they wanted to open up, most felt the weight of duty. They knew the wrong word might cost their employees their jobs, and their shareholders billions. That they opened up at all was as much a credit to their own courage as to any skill of the interviewer. In the end, they really are true heroes.

It was the interview with Kim Polese that changed my thinking and gave the title to this series.

Kim, shattered by family tragedy, had bravely agreed to stick to her scheduled interview, knowing full well that it would pick at this fresh wound in her heart. In fact, she seemed to grow stronger as the interview went on.

Then, while answering a simple background question about her years at Sun Microsystems marketing the Java programming language, she suddenly, almost offhandedly, made a remark that seemed to distill everything I had ever learned about entrepreneurs and their lives. She said, simply, "I realized I was willing to die for Java."

There it was.

Having met hundreds of entrepreneurs of every color, nationality, sexual persuasion, and religion—men and women whose personalities ranged from charismatic to poisonous, blowhard to taciturn, beatific to sociopathic—I had already abandoned my most basic preconceptions about how an entrepreneur should look and behave. And thanks to the interviews in this series, I was also beginning to formulate something new and important about how entrepreneurs meet the world.

Now Kim brought it all together for me. Ask me now what an entrepreneur is, and I will tell you, with the hesitancy of someone who has seen most of his cherished beliefs on the subject destroyed: An entrepreneur is a person who has an overwhelming need to control and organize his or her life. So profound is this need, and so deep is the commitment, that the entrepreneur is willing to bet everything, including that life, to reach that goal.

Notice that this definition says nothing about business. And, indeed, entrepreneurs can be found in every corner of society, from politics to entertainment to nonprofit institutions. Only in business, especially technology business, does the title normally attach.

But the definition itself only raises more questions—one in particular: What makes people willing to risk everything for such an impossible goal? The answer, or at least the beginning of an answer, can be found in the pages of this book. Some entrepreneurs, I think, carry deep childhood scars, unbearable memories of moments when their entire universe spun out of control—and they have spent the rest of their lives fighting to make sure that never happens to them again. Others, I think, are simply natural entrepreneurs—equipped from birth with both the ego and the will to go it solo through life. And a third group—one might call them the shrewd entrepreneurs—came to a point in their careers when they realized, sometimes reluctantly, that the only way forward was alone, armed with only their skill and wit.

You'll find examples of each type in the pages to come. Perhaps you may even find yourself. After all, for each of us there is something for which we are willing to bet it all.

Betting It All

Jerry Sanders
Founder, Chairman, and CEO, Advanced Micro Devices

The Man
- Born on September 12, 1936
- Raised in Chicago, Illinois
- Educated at the University of Illinois
- Remarried, three children

The Entrepreneur
- The quintessential company builder
- Founded AMD in 1969 and battled industry giants in developing it into a leading semiconductor manufacturer
- AMD year 2000 revenues: $4.6 billion (fiscal year ending 12/31/00)

"I remember one of my professors saying, 'Jerry, you have great capability. Don't be a dilettante. Focus on something. You can make a real contribution.' Well, I didn't make the kind of contribution that he thought as far as being a scientist, but I never forgot that. Focus on something important, and stay with it."

*J*erry Sanders's arrival at the studio was all that you would expect from a man whose nickname is "Hollywood."

W.J. (Jerry) Sanders III, as the flamboyant salesman for Fairchild in southern California, was already a legend before his 25th birthday. He lived perpetually beyond his means, mythically wore pink trousers on a sales call to buttoned-down IBM, raced around in a convertible Bentley, squired beautiful women — and became the first symbol of the high-living side of tech tycoonship.

Forty years on, little had apparently changed. Sanders swept into the studio as if it were a royal visit. With a great shock of silver hair, an impeccably tailored suit, a diamond bezeled Rolex, and a phalanx of crisp young assistants, Sanders rolled over makeup people, studio technicians, and everyone else in his path.

But Jerry Sanders is an infinitely more complex figure than his reputation suggests. A hint of that can be seen in the studio photograph. Note that Sanders was the only guest who sat in the opposite seat, the one I normally used. The reason wasn't just vanity, but practicality: Sanders's nose was so badly broken by gang members as a teenager that he still cannot look easily to his left.

But read his words as well. Jerry Sanders is not merely a super-salesman who made good with his own company. Both marketing guru Regis McKenna and legendary Intel founder (and competitor) Bob Noyce called Sanders the smartest man in Silicon Valley.

As the youngest and most outrageous of the chip industry's pioneers, Sanders has always been underestimated. Where the founders of Intel located start-up funding in a matter of hours, Sanders's search for investors in Advanced Micro Devices took months, reducing him to sleeping on a friend's couch. Thus, from the beginning, he was forced to play perpetual catch-up with his giant counterpart. It was a role he had now played for nearly three decades, through good times and bad and through one of the most expensive and protracted business lawsuits in history.

Thus, for all of his showbiz manner, there was something deeply poignant about the Jerry Sanders who sat across from me that day. He was no longer the brash young man with a dream, but was now a scarred old warrior, the last of his generation. All his peers had died or retired rich; Sanders fought on. The man who, more than anyone in American business, always seemed to be playing at being a CEO now admitted to me in a devastating remark that it "was no longer fun."

This was to be his last hurrah. AMD had just introduced its Athlon microprocessor chip, its final great salvo aimed at Intel's hegemony. Athlon would make or break the company—and Jerry Sanders. Our interview was shot beneath the specter of that enormous wager.

As for the shoot itself, it was something of a bittersweet reunion. In 1983 I interviewed Sanders in depth for my first book, a history of Silicon Valley. The result was a profile that changed forever the industry's view of Sanders. But his candidness had cost him much. It severed forever his relationship with his mother. As

Sanders sat down in my chair, he was understandably wary. I wondered, given our history, just how open he'd be.

I needn't have worried. Within minutes I was in the grip of a master.

※

I've followed your career for an awful long time. And there's these two giant millstones sitting out there. One of them's called Microsoft. The other one's called Intel. And anybody who's gotten in their path has been either crushed under them or crushed between them. But not you. And you're sort of like Ishmael. You know, "I alone survived to tell the tale." Why you?

Well, I tell you, I think first of all, it's character. I think, you know, what it's all about really is character and commitment. You know, when I look for a leader in my business, when I look for a guy I want to give an important position to or a responsibility to, the first thing I go for is character. The second thing I go for is commitment and accountability. Then I look for basically leadership skills, and then what is the skills set? I like to talk about character, commitment, capability, and then competitiveness.

I love to travel. I love the south of France. I love wonderful cars. I love the good life. But the reality is, there's a part of me which is duty driven. And I am determined to fulfill my dream at AMD.

I think that drive came from my upbringing in Chicago. My grandfather and my grandmother were good, God-fearing people.

My grandmother was the most loving, wonderful person until I was 13 years old, because my mother and father divorced when I was quite young. And about the time I was 4 or 5, my grandparents—my paternal grandparents—raised me. And my mother and father remarried and each had five children with their second mates, leaving me and one brother as sort of the abandoned mistakes of the first marriage.

My grandmother was very happy to raise me when I was a little boy—right up until about the time that I was replaced by my father's first son from his second wife, at which time [it became] much more desirable to be a grandmother to a one-year-old than to a pimply-faced adolescent rebel, questioning everything that he'd ever been taught, which is about what I was when I got to high school.

My brother—my one full-blood brother—was raised by my maternal grandmother on a policeman's widow's pension. So we literally grew up in entirely different environments. My grandfather was the assistant electrical engineer for the city of Chicago and had a great belief that good things only came from hard work.

My grandfather was an unusual human being. He got a college degree at a school called Armour Institute, which is now the Illinois Institute of Technology. Of course, in those days, the only thing they dealt with was direct current, so he had a much more limited curriculum than I did.

My grandfather did not have any of his children complete college. He always felt that they had given up too soon. My grandfather was a very harsh taskmaster. He'd never give you any encouragement. I mean, on public television, I can't use the words he used to say, but basically he said, "You're a shanty Irishman. You'll wind up nothing more than a pile of you-know-what."

And I thought, "Gee, that's a great, encouraging thing." So I guess my first motivation was to show my grandfather he was wrong, and I was going to be a heck of a lot more than he ever thought.

My grandfather told me if I didn't go to school, I was worth less than dirt. And he didn't care what I studied in school as long as it was something I could make a living at. And his definition of making a living was [to] be an engineer. You can get a job. You can make money. You can survive, and you won't be a drag on me as you have been for [the] entire 21 years of your life.

R e c k o n i n g

When I graduated from college, no one came to my graduation. Nobody would even go so far as the University of Illinois in Champaign-Urbana, a scant 120-mile drive away. And when I came home, my grandfather presented me with a bill. And it was a listing of all of the canned goods and charges for the laundry my grandmother had done for me, which I used to send home from college. This is how much he felt I owed him, and he hoped I would pay it back when I was able.

It made me laugh because it was just so outrageous. How could my grandfather do that? I knew in his own way he loved me. I knew he was proud of me. And I think what I was most impressed with was [that] he kept such meticulous records. I thought, "God, he's not even a Virgo."

I n d i f f e r e n t   H o n o r s

I was a very good student, but I wasn't a very serious student. I got good grades and was valedictorian of my high school class. I graduated with honors from the University of Illinois, and I never took a lab class. I never took a lab class, and so the only grade—the only time I never got an A or a B was if there was a lab. I think I got two C's—maybe I only got one C in college. I only remember one C in power engineering, [about] which I said, "Look, I'm not going to go to a Saturday lab class." And the professor told me, "If you don't go to lab, you will not get better than a C, no matter how well you do on the exams." And I disbelieved him. I did well, but it turns out he was right. He gave me a C. I remembered that. So I learned my lesson.

What I wanted was to be rich and famous and have beautiful women on my arm, which is all we can really say on television. I wanted to be Ty Hardin, the cowboy actor.

I didn't know what I wanted to do. I mean, who knows what they want to do when they're in their teens? You know, I just knew I wanted a better life.

I was always quite quick with the quip or the remark, which caused me [on] a number of occasions to get into fights with people who were bigger and stronger than I was.

I started working out and trying to get more physically fit so I could better defend myself. And in so doing, I learned about Santa Monica's Muscle Beach. And I thought, "Gee, I'd like to take a trip to Muscle Beach."

Way out West

So, when I was in my midteens, I went to Santa Monica Muscle Beach. And I wasn't so much interested in Muscle Beach as I was interested in, "Wow, southern California's phenomenal. What a great place to live."

What I really liked about it was the transparent society. In Chicago, where I went to school, everybody knew what your background must be. If you went to Lindblom High School on the south side of Chicago, everyone knew that you didn't have the same background as someone who went to New Trier High School in Winnetka. And I didn't like that. You were automatically classified. My grandfather was adamant about diction and grammar, pointing out that people could tell where you were from by how you talked and how you spoke. My neighborhood was a "dese," "dem," and "dose" neighborhood.

We were the lace-curtain house in the neighborhood. My grandmother kept a very fine house, and my grandfather permitted no "dese," "dem," or "dose" in our house. So I wanted to go to California, because I thought it would be a great place to live.

I had my childhood fantasies that someday I'd—maybe I could be an actor. I actually was introduced to somebody who could have been very influential—a woman who was a widow of an important movie producer. And I probably could have used her influence to become an actor if she wouldn't have discouraged me by pointing out to me that what did I possibly have going for me that would make an actor?

She said, "You know, I was just talking to a fine young man, and he's 10 times better looking than you are, and he can't even get a job." And his name was Efrem Zimbalist Jr. I'll never forget that day. And I thought, "Wow." Later on in life, when *77 Sunset Strip* was a big deal and Efrem Zimbalist Jr. was one of the stars, I said, "You know what? She's wrong. He's 100 times better looking than I am." So she said, "About the only thing you could be, Jerry, is a cowboy." And so I said, "Well, you know . . ." I wasn't sure I wanted to do that.

Bad Blood

One of the reasons why Efrem Zimbalist Jr. was 10 times better looking than I was because my nose had gotten messed up in a pretty severe fight. It's kind of funny, you know, a few years ago, I was in Hong Kong, and I took the time to go to one of these for-tune-tellers. You know, it was kind of fun. And the fortune-teller told me that I had two lifelines. And one of them went on for a very long time, possibly even to the century mark. It was a little obscure. But the other lifeline ended when I was 18. And what happened to me when I was 18?

At 18, I was at a party. I was home from college, and I went to a high school football game. And, of course, I was no longer in high school, but it was at the—a team of the school I had gone to. And I was there with a couple of guys that I didn't know really well who had been football players when I was there.

Before the Bentley: Even at a young age, Jerry Sanders dreamed of a Hollywood career.

I went with those guys to a party afterwards. And this party, unfortunately, was dominated by a gang. The gang's name was the Chi Nine, which obviously stands for the Chicago Nine. And I didn't know anything about the Chi Nine, but one of the guys I was with had a high degree of interest in a girl who was at the party who happened to be presumably the property of the leader of the Chi Nine.

This leader—I'm never going to forget this guy's name—it was Bob Biocek. And Bob Biocek decided he was going to fight with my friend. And my friend went outside, and they started fighting. And it wasn't going particularly well for either one of them. And so Bob Biocek, the gang leader, decided to have a few friends help him finish off my friend.

There were four or five of them. And I—again, because of my character—jumped in to help him. I really thought that I could make a difference. To my surprise, my friend ran off and escaped and left me there, and these guys decided, well, I was the next best thing to him. So they did me up pretty well. They broke my nose, fractured my skull, kicked in my ribs, carved me up with a beer can. Fortunately, I had a coat on so it didn't make any lasting scars on my back. And they dumped me in a garbage can, which I thought was a pretty nasty thing to do. I look back now, it's amazing I survived that.

Fortunately, one of the guys at the party was a next-door neighbor. And he put me in the trunk of his car, having extracted me from the garbage can, took me to the Little Company of Mary Hospital on 95th in Evergreen Park, and dropped me off at the emergency section, saying, "He was in a car accident." Well, of course, I wasn't, but there I was, unconscious with a fractured skull. So they put me in the emergency ward.

And to make a long story short, they gave me the last rites. And a few days later I came out of the coma, and there I was with my skull caved in. It looked like somebody had actually taken a silver dollar and impressed it in the center of my forehead and just pounded it in there.

Fortunately, it's gotten a little better, but I've always had this broken nose and always have to look from left to right instead of right to left.

Direction

It was a turning point in my life. What I remember most about that was that I'd been betrayed by a friend. And he wasn't my best friend. He wasn't a guy I knew that well. But I'd gone to help him. And my reward for that was he let me down. He let me down big time.

And I thought about it afterwards. I saw him afterwards. He told me he had a broken jaw from a football injury, and his jaw was wired. He could have really been hurt if he'd stuck around.

And I looked at this guy and I thought, "This is just ridiculous. You let me down. You copped out. I went to your aid, and you betrayed me."

It taught me a couple of things. Number one, it taught me, you know, maybe you shouldn't always count on people that you don't know. That's where this character thing comes in. Character really counts to me. This guy showed no character whatsoever. Number two, it taught me that life isn't fair. And I've become an advocate of fairness in everything.

I remember that when these guys were rounded up—and I guess it was the district attorney or the city attorney [who] was going to prosecute—he said, "You know, there's no real point in prosecuting. These guys are already all out on probation. Their families have no money so there's no way to get any money from them." In fact, in those days, it never even occurred to us to sue for damages other than maybe to get the medical bills paid. Instead, my grandfather once again had to pay, which was unfortunate. The attorney said, "These are just bad guys. So we'll get a guilty plea, but they'll just get more probation. They'll just extend their probation." There's no justice. I didn't think that was fair.

But there was justice eventually. Bob Biocek was found dead in a Denver street fight seven years later. I had nothing to do with it, although in some of my more romantic moments, if that's the right word—maybe not romantic, but fantastic—I thought of writing a fictionalized account of my life where I had something to do with it.

Mongrel

I've never let myself be burdened with negativity. I think it just drags you down. I think, learn from your mistakes, learn from your experiences, and move forward.

I think I've always been kind of optimistic. I think I've been—I'm a great believer in the American dream. You know, it turns out, as I say, I'm kind of a mongrel. I'm Swedish, Scotch, Irish, and German. There are a lot of ethnicities in there. All of those ethnicities came from immigrants—a general contractor from Sweden and a laborer from Ireland, among others. And they all came to America, and they made a better life. That's why I think America's just the greatest place in the world.

[In 1959 Jerry Sanders joined the legendary Fairchild Semiconductor, the pioneering chip company and the founding firm of modern Silicon Valley.]

Just thinking about Fairchild—it was just incredible. There's never been anything like it before. There will never be anything like it since. It could have survived.

Despite the stories, I wasn't too wild for Fairchild. I was too wild for Les Hogan (then president of Fairchild). It turns out Fairchild was doing just great. They had become the number one producer of integrated circuits in the world. They rocketed up to $100 million a year. Texas Instruments (TI) had been caught flat-footed. TI was the big man on campus. Fairchild was the one. We had won the contract for the North American Aviation-Autonetics division program for the Minuteman missile. And then TI took it back with just brute force and market power.

In the end, Fairchild didn't betray me, but Les Hogan did. But people make mistakes. He's told me later that he regretted it—it was the biggest mistake he ever made in his professional life, but, yeah, he fired me. Again, here I am at Fairchild doing a great job, albeit with a certain number of detractors, because again I had not quite gotten control of the things I said. I was an iconoclast. When the emperor had no clothes, I was the first one to point it out.

Fairchild was not getting adequate funding and support from its corporate parent. And that's what caused so many people to leave Fairchild. I believe that had Fairchild rewarded its contributors appropriately, they could have kept enough of that team together to make Fairchild more than the combined Intel, AMD, and National Semiconductor today. If I could have run it, it would have made it. They should have given me a chance. I was a baby when I started AMD, too, and I made it happen, and they said it couldn't be done.

When I was fired from Fairchild, it was crucial to me that, first and foremost, I demonstrate to myself that they were wrong. You know, I think there's always been a little bit of insecurity in me, probably always will be. And I did wonder, "Were they right? Was Les right? Was I the wrong guy to lead the marketing organization of an industry-leading technology company?" I think I knew he was wrong when AMD went public.

Doing It the Hard Way

From the beginning, it's been a grunt. I mean, I don't know what made me decide that my life should always be about making love standing up in a hammock, but this is the way that my life has worked out.

Thirty years is a pretty good focus. You know, I have to say, "I carried deferred gratification to a ridiculous limit."

If I met a young Jerry Sanders today, my advice to him would be to pay at least as much attention to the base camp as he does to climbing the mountain. I've been blessed by having had two wonderful wives in my life. I had a wife for a long time, gave me three wonderful children. I think the pressures of business contributed substantially to the dissolution of that marriage. But the realities are, it turned out to be a blessing, because I've stayed close to my kids, and it's allowed me to meet a new woman, fall in love, get married, and have this incredible second family.

So, I guess what I would tell the guy [is] pay attention to base camp. And that goes [for] now. So I've got to pay attention to my base camp. Now, I'm still out climbing mountains. And I intend to continue to climb the mountain. But I'm paying attention to my base camp.

When I worked for Fairchild, I worked with a guy named Don Valentine. *[Valentine is now the dean of Silicon Valley venture capitalists.]* And Don said something a long time ago. What gave him pleasure was collecting stock certificates in a safe deposit box. And I looked at him and I thought, "Wow, that wouldn't give me any pleasure at all." What I liked was collecting experiences.

And so the reason I'm a fun guy or have been a fun guy is I like traveling the world. I enjoy going to our plants in Penang. I enjoy going to the south of France. Who wouldn't? I enjoyed going out to the countryside outside of London and bidding on antiques. I enjoy experiences. What I regret is that I don't have more free time. I'm not having much fun right now. Not professionally, I'm not having much fun.

≋

In February 2001, Jerry Sanders at last announced his retirement from the leadership of Advanced Micro Devices for an effective date that has since been extended to April 2002. The months between the shoot and his announcement had proven to be happy ones. The Athlon chip, after a slow start, found itself with a perfect market opportunity. It was not only more powerful than Intel's latest Pentium chip, but the giant company seemed momentarily confused. Customers, meanwhile, were happy to adopt an alternative that would counter Intel's market dominance.

Thus, by the beginning of 2001, AMD was rolling up unprecedented market share. Revenues were booming, even in a down market. And Jerry Sanders, at long last, could declare victory. He had finally proven himself to the generations of naysayers. Now he could go home to Hollywood and have fun again.

Photo by Ted Betz

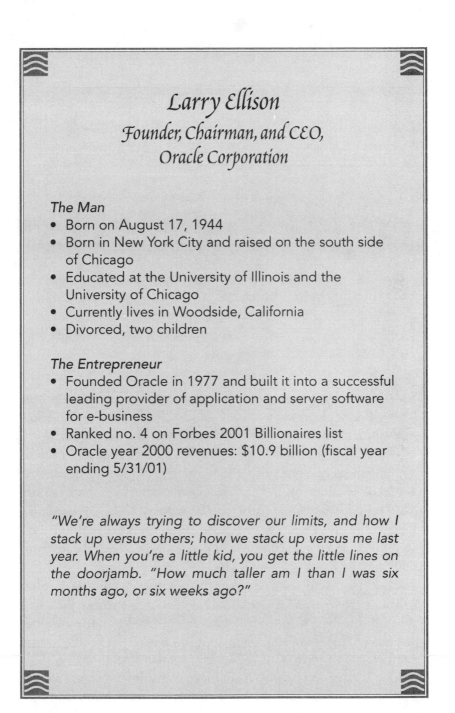

Larry Ellison
Founder, Chairman, and CEO, Oracle Corporation

The Man
- Born on August 17, 1944
- Born in New York City and raised on the south side of Chicago
- Educated at the University of Illinois and the University of Chicago
- Currently lives in Woodside, California
- Divorced, two children

The Entrepreneur
- Founded Oracle in 1977 and built it into a successful leading provider of application and server software for e-business
- Ranked no. 4 on Forbes 2001 Billionaires list
- Oracle year 2000 revenues: $10.9 billion (fiscal year ending 5/31/01)

"We're always trying to discover our limits, and how I stack up versus others; how we stack up versus me last year. When you're a little kid, you get the little lines on the doorjamb. "How much taller am I than I was six months ago, or six weeks ago?"

One story from the shoot tells you something important about Larry Ellison, chairman and CEO of Oracle Corporation, and, for a few months recently, the world's wealthiest private citizen.

Like Bill Gates and Scott McNealy, Ellison's people insisted that we tape at his company's studios, hidden behind the giant, Oz-like glass cylinders of the Oracle's headquarters complex beside San Francisco Bay. But unlike with Gates or McNealy, the negotiating didn't end there. Ann McAdam soon found herself in a cat-and-mouse game with Ellison's PR people, who changed dates and times and demanded different kinds of editorial control.

Luckily, McAdam is tougher than any corporate flack. She held her ground, and eventually Oracle caved. Perhaps that had always been their plan, and they merely wanted to put us on the defensive. That's how things are done at Oracle.

We arrived to find, as expected, a state-of-the-art studio. But there was none of the crisp casualness we would see at Microsoft. Rather, like almost everything else at Oracle, there was a palpable tension in the air. Ellison, as usual, was late—one hour late—

leaving us once again to wonder if it was merely another way to get an edge.

So we settled into the greenroom to await the Great Man. Around us, as the minutes passed, the tension level slowly rose until the air had the fevered feel of a room of courtiers sweating out the imminent appearance of a volatile potentate. Bob Grove, Ann, and I, by contrast, put our feet up and munched granola bars from a snack tray. But even as we ate, an object in the corner of the room made us increasingly curious. It was another tray, identical to ours but covered with a white tablecloth. Finally, curiosity overcame me. I walked over and started to lift a corner of the cloth.

"Don't touch that!" ordered a voice from another corner of the room. I turned; it was one of the flacks. "I'm sorry," she said, "but that's Larry's tray"—as if that was all that needed to be said.

Now I had to know. Caviar? Lark's tongues in aspic? A few minutes later, after the PR person had left the room, I walked back over, lifted the cloth . . . and saw the same collection of granola bars, muffins, fruit, and cookies as on the other tray. Apparently, Ellison just didn't eat with mortals.

Finally, Ellison arrived with his retinue. He seemed to appear out of nowhere, as swift and purposeful as a shark. He said a few words to his people, then dropped into the chair, adjusting his lapels as he did. His appearance—in his tailored suit, with his well-groomed hair and skin and manicured beard—was as always, perfect. Knowing that Ellison would likely depart as quickly as he had arrived, I began the interview immediately, with almost no preparatory small talk.

The image of Larry Ellison is that of a tough guy; however, he is anything but. As a former investigative reporter—and as the son of a military officer and spook—I've seen my share of tough guys. Ellison is not one of them. Rather, he is a very smart, overgrown 15-year-old with scars from very deep wounds. He would talk about those wounds during the interview—the aunt who was, in fact, his mother, his life on the streets of Chicago—with a jaunty style that did little to camouflage the hurt.

Somehow those wounds were converted into a relentless ambition. But the scars never went away. And when Larry Ellison found himself rich almost beyond imagining, he decided to live out every one of his long-frustrated 15-year-old's fantasies: fighter pilot, sailor, Don Juan, James Bond, samurai, tycoon. The lost little boy has taken on a persona that few of the rest of us can even imagine, much less inhabit. It is an enviable life, but one not likely envied by many adults.

If that sounds like psychoanalysis, forgive me, but when interviewing Ellison you find yourself filled with such a complicated and contradictory collection of emotions—pity, admiration, revulsion, curiosity, sympathy, and fear—that you can't help but puzzle out afterwards what you just saw.

The interview itself? I'll leave that for you to judge. I was just holding on as I went down the rabbit hole. At times Ellison seemed vulnerable: Tears filled his eyes when he spoke of his lost Oracle partner, Bob Minor. Other times he gave brief glimpses of why he has a reputation for cruelty and narcissism. And yet at other moments, as when talking about his early days in the industry or his near fatal yacht race, he seemed a man who'd faced his limitations and been humbled by them. Yet from the moment he walked into the studio to the instant he left, threat seemed to encircle him like a penumbra.

Which is the real Larry Ellison? Probably all of them. If he is a ball of contradictions, then that is probably what it took to go as far as he has with the material he had to work with. All I know is that driving home that night I was vastly relieved to see the Oracle towers receding in my rearview mirror. I had survived my one-on-one with Larry Ellison.

I'm curious about some things. I've been covering the Valley for 30 years, so one of the things that intrigues me about you is why

would somebody with so much to lose take so many damn risks? I mean, I watched you in the Sydney/Hobart Race, and I thought, "My God, why is he out there? People are getting killed."

We had sailed into a hurricane when a storm was forecast. These are all very precise terms when it comes to weather and sailing. A storm is about 40 knots of breeze, and we got about twice that, which is—the name for that isn't "storm," the name for that is "hurricane." We found ourselves in the middle of a terrible hurricane, enormous waves—and not only were the waves tall, but they were extremely steep. Driving into one of those waves was like driving into an office building made of water. The bow of the boat would just dig into the wave, and you would be washed off the wheel, and people would go flying across the deck.

And that wasn't the worst part of it. The worst part of it is that you go up the up elevator of the wave, as buoyancy carries you. Normally, when you reach the top of a wave, you start sliding down the back—you start surfing, actually. Your boat starts surfing, and that's actually very dangerous. We didn't do that. The boat simply exited—the wave—the backs of the waves were so steep, we simply exited the wave and started falling.

We went airborne for one one-thousand, two one-thousand, three one-thousand, slam, into the deck. The yacht's 80 feet long, and she's out of the water, and she's falling. The surface tension of the water is such that when you hit, it's like falling onto asphalt. So about every 45 seconds, we were dropped off a four-story building onto asphalt. We wondered if the boat was going to hold together. The guys on the bow would simply leave the bow. The boat would start falling, and the guys would be suspended in midair. Then, when the boat hit and started coming back up again, it would catch the guys as they were still falling down. We had four guys with broken bones, a couple very seriously injured. No one died on our boat. That wasn't true for all the boats. Fifty-five guys went in the water and if it wasn't for the insane heroics of the Australian Navy, going out there to pull those people out of the water, it wouldn't have been 6 dead, it would have been 55 dead.

Why did I do it? I think because we're endlessly curious about ourselves. When Edmund Hillary was asked that famous line about why did he climb Everest, and he said, "Because it was there," that's simply not true. He climbed the mountain because *he* was there and he was curious if he could do it. We're always curious about each other, and we're curious about ourselves.

I did break my neck bodysurfing once. I was actually on the big island, and there was a storm. They weren't allowing anyone to take T boards out. So I was out there with three young Hawaiian guys, and we're just diving through these huge waves. Then this enormous wave showed up and I was in the perfect position to catch it, so I just decided to bodysurf the wave. And for about the first half second it was very exciting; thereafter, it was terrifying.

I just accelerated off the wave. I've surfed a bunch and I've never felt any kind of acceleration like off that wave. There's no continental shelf—there's no shallowing as you get closer to the shore in Hawaii—so the waves come in much faster than they do here in California. The wave took me down and buried me into the reef. I broke my neck in two places, I broke my collarbone, and I broke a few ribs and punctured a lung. It was awful.

Actually, I had no intention of surfing that wave. I was just in the perfect spot to catch the perfect wave. There was something in me that wanted to ride that wave. I think that is a fundamental personality trait of mine, which is to be, I guess in the worst sense, *reckless*, both in business and in sports.

Where's it come from? I don't know. There are biology books which say that it's actually genetic. Who knows? I don't know if it's a family trait or not. My sister is quoted as saying I've been trying to kill myself since I was a kid. I think I'm getting better at it [*laughs*].

There's a wonderful book out by Melvin Konner, who wrote the Harvard sociobiology textbook called *The Tangled Wing*. One of the books he wrote was *Why the Reckless Survive*. You would think if there was a trait among us that would disappear, it would be recklessness—that, eventually, reckless people would kill themselves off before they got to the breeding stage. That Darwin would kind of clean up the gene pool and get rid of the reckless gene.

In fact, there are tremendous rewards for recklessness. It was the reckless guy in the village who went out in the middle of the snowstorm and killed the buffalo and brought back meat to feed the rest of the village. It was the reckless guy in the computer industry who decided that, when everyone said a relational database would never be commercially viable, said, "Well, maybe everyone's wrong—maybe I will take a chance with my career and with my cash."

It's not a rational process. I think we want to keep learning our entire lives, and we want to keep learning about ourselves our entire lives. It's not a K-through-12 or K-through-college thing. It's a life of endless discovery, part of it personal, part of it external, part of it in business, and part of it outside of business. I think it's a lifestyle and a curiosity that stays with you forever.

Mean Streets

I was born in New York and raised in Chicago. My mother wasn't married; I was born when she was very young. She and my grandmother took care of me for the first nine months. I got pneumonia and nearly died. It was very traumatic for everyone—I'm sure for me, too, though I was nine months old and really don't remember. Eventually, I was adopted within my own family. I was actually adopted by my maternal aunt. So my grandmother's sister in Chicago and her husband raised me.

When I was nine months old I moved from New York to Chicago. I found out that I was adopted when I was about 11 or 12 years old. I found out it was within my own family when I was considerably older.

I lived in a poor, rough neighborhood. My sister has another wonderful line that says, "The richer I am now, the poorer we were as kids. *[Laughs.]* It was a lower-middle-class neighborhood. But it wasn't rough by today's standards. It was a series of ghettos—a Hispanic ghetto, a black ghetto, a Jewish ghetto—and I didn't know it was a poor neighborhood. I didn't know it was a rough neighborhood. It was the only thing I really knew.

I saw my natural mother once growing up, but I didn't know it was my mother. We took a trip to New York City and I met her, not knowing who she was.

The truth of the matter is, it did make me feel a bit of an outsider inside of my own family because, in fact, I didn't know my adopted family was also related to these people. When I was 12, I just knew that I was adopted—from whom, I had no idea.

I knew, probably, when I was 25, that I was adopted within my own family. But I didn't really go searching for my biological mother until the two people who had raised me passed away. I could get into a long conversation as to why I didn't, but I didn't. When I finally went ahead and pursued the search and found her, the result was surprising to me, because my reaction was: I really found out who my family was, and it was the people who raised me, not the people who I was biologically related to. I'm not sure you ever really know how your adoption affects you.

My adopted father was, when he was young, a bomber pilot in the war. Actually, he led squadrons over the terrible bombing of Dresden. But early on in World War II, he had a squadron of all women pilots, ferrying airplanes from the United States to England. When they had enough planes there, they gave him the bad news. They had plenty of airplanes, but a shortage of pilots. So, "You're staying." And, "You're no longer a ferry pilot; you're now going to be a squadron leader."

After the war, he actually ran for political office and made a lot of money in real estate, but eventually he lost everything. After that, he worked for the federal government as an auditor. He became very, very conservative, about as risk-averse as you can get.

I challenged authority from an early age. Mark Twain defines an expert as just some guy from out of town. That's the way I felt

Sailor samurai: Larry Ellison's yacht, racing before the wind.

about my teachers and experts and conventional wisdom: Unless you explain to me why this is true, just because the "expert" says it's true, I didn't reflexively obey.

I did very well in science and math, but I certainly was not a straight A student. I had a lot of problems in school. I remember correcting and getting into a big argument with a math teacher. I had a very difficult time with people who said, "Do what I say—I'm the adult, you're the kid."

Dropping Out

I started off at the University of Illinois and spent a little time there. I tested well, but my grades were very checkered. I had a lot of A's and I had a lot of things that were definitely not A's.

I was a physics/math major in college. Then I left the University of Illinois and I went to the University of Chicago for a while. You know, I'm a college dropout. I was at Illinois for a couple of years and Chicago for a year. And that seemed like more than enough for me.

When I was in college, I learned how to program. That's one of the things you did in math and physics in those days—you programmed. You wrote programs to conduct your experiments.

I contracted myself out as a programmer. I found out that I was very, very fast. I would watch how long people would take to do things. And I would start fixed-price bidding jobs and get the job done very, very quickly. I found that I was making more than some of my professors, working part-time as a programmer.

Writing code was very gamelike and hyperrational. The computer did exactly what you told it to do. There was no ambiguity at all, and I've always had problems with ambiguities and authority.

In 1967, I left college and came to California because California is where it was all happening. I left Chicago and drove to Berkeley and was living in Berkeley in my "lost 20s." But I never wore beads. So I'd like to get that straight now. In fact, my friends who were all wearing beads in those days in the '60s tried to get me to put on what were then called "love beads." I had a good lottery number so [I] missed being drafted.

I bummed around as a contract programmer for a while and then Silicon Valley just began to grow. I stopped doing contract programming and started working at Amdahl when the company was just started; then Gene Amdahl left IBM to create the world's fastest mainframe computer.

I was a hotshot programmer and programming was an absolute meritocracy. You could be a high school dropout, but if you could code, it didn't really make any difference. You didn't have to wear a tie or have enormous academic credentials. If you were a good programmer, you got the job.

Interestingly enough, what I learned from Gene Amdahl was to never, ever take venture capital, because they fired him. Gene was a brilliant guy. I'm going to make a lot of my venture capitalist friends very unhappy, but I used to go around making speeches called "Just Say No to Venture Capital." The venture capitalists, at least in those days, had a terrible track record of bringing people in and then throwing the entrepreneur out. That's usually a terrible mistake.

Start-up Stumble

We started Oracle in 1977. Bob Minor, Ed Oates, Bruce Scott, and I—there were four of us who really started the company. We started with $2,000. I put in the bulk of the capital, 1,200 bucks, and we started doing consulting. We wanted to build the first commercial relational database, but the only way we could pay for it was to hire ourselves out as programmers. And we were pretty good programmers, so we could make money doing contract work.

We had a little, tiny office in Santa Clara. I think there are pictures of us nailing up our sign—it was then called Software Development Laboratories, SDL.

I had a mortgage at the time. What's worse, I had a mortgage, I was married, and I was building a house. And the Bank of America—the old Bank of America, the one headquartered in San Francisco, not in North Carolina—foreclosed on both of them.

Don Lucas has been a venture capitalist for, I think, 40 years; he is one of the deans of venture capital. We were in the same building as Don. We had moved out of our Santa Clara offices, and when my houses were being foreclosed, we were in offices at 3000 Sand Hill Road, which is now the capital of venture capital. So we were having lunch with the venture capitalists; we just weren't taking their money.

Bob Minor told Don that my houses were being foreclosed on. I was president of the company, and I'd stopped paying myself first, so I couldn't make payments on the houses, and the bank didn't like that. So Don kind of wandered down into my office and said, "Larry, how are things going?" I said, "Great, Don, great." He said, "Well, how're you doing financially? Everything okay?" I said, "Fabulous, no problems."

Finally, I realized that Bob had told Don. Don loaned me the money to pay my mortgages. He said, "You really shouldn't be worrying about that. You should just be worrying about the company. You have an amazing company here—amazing potential with this company. You shouldn't be distracted by a personal financial crisis."

I really didn't think there was a risk in starting the business. What was I risking? My current job? Sure I was risking my house, but given the potential upside—well, I could always go out and get a great job. I was eminently employable. Even in those days, it would take about an hour to get a pretty good job in Silicon Valley. It wasn't a big risk. So the trade-offs were obvious.

Bob Minor was an incredible guy. He passed away; he died of cancer. He was probably the nicest guy I ever met. I think we were both good programmers, and our personalities were very different.

I remember Bob coming to me one time and saying that one of our employees was getting divorced, and he was losing half of his stock options to his soon-to-be-ex-wife in the settlement; therefore, we should give this guy more stock options. And I asked jokingly, "What about raising his salary to cover his child support?" Bob said, "Good idea!"

Bob loved the people in the company and was almost an irrational advocate. I mean, an irrational advocate of how the people are far more important than the business. That was clear to everybody, and he was very popular.

I miss Bob as a friend. But Bob dropped out of the business long before he got ill. Bob was really gone from the business, so in terms of us working side by side and moving forward, that had ceased—that relationship was long gone. But our friendship was tremendously important, and the history we had together was tremendously important. I loved Bob a lot; I really miss him as a friend.

Pulling out of the Dive

We saw Oracle having about 50 employees, and we have 43,000 now. The goal of starting the company was that I wanted to make a comfortable living. But the primary goal was to control my own environment. I wasn't happy working for other people. I wasn't happy working on projects I didn't find interesting, working with people I didn't enjoy spending time with. So it really was an environmental control system I was trying to create, where I'd enjoy going to work everyday, and enjoy the people I was working with, and enjoy the projects I was working on, and make a decent living. There was never a goal, really, to become rich, let alone create a pretty large company.

The size of the company today and the wealth—it's surreal. It stuns me now. It's a long way from the south side of Chicago. As my sister said, "I really don't get it—I was the smart one!" [*Laughs*] I think my family is like me. I can't believe it; neither can they.

1991 and '92 were difficult years at Oracle. I had to ask myself, "Am I going to stay in charge of this place, or is it best for the company for me to get out?" And I kept the job. I wanted to keep the job because I thought I was best qualified to repair the damage that I'd caused.

We got to a point where the company was getting out of control. This is going to sound like me making excuses, but I've always run engineering. The part of the company that I'm really interested in and the part of the company that Bob was interested in was engineering. Now, we had a really large company, and I had no experience in running one. I was getting my experience on the job, and, boy, the tuition was a lot higher than what you pay for Stanford business school. I had no experience running anything this big, and no one had any experience in growing a company this fast. This was all uncharted territory for me, personally and in the history of commerce.

We had no numbers guy, in fact, and we had a field sales organization that was—I guess the positive term you would use is "aggressive." It was a very, very aggressive selling organization. And there were no controls in place.

Normally, you have a chief financial officer who is making sure that certain procedures and protocols are in place, so there are no abuses going on out in the field. We had none of that. I didn't even know you're supposed to have that. I was spending most of my time worrying about products. Today, I worry about it all.

As I came to understand the problems anew every day, it was a horrible experience, because I had been paying no attention to the field, or finance.

Self-deception is powerful stuff. But as I looked around, I saw outside managers brought into a lot of companies who then made things dramatically worse. The French fired Napoleon—there was no worse HR decision in history.

I think I was the best person for the job. I think I knew the company better than anybody else. I knew the products and the technology and the markets that we were in better than anybody else.

I certainly took a lot of long walks alone. It was always Yosemite, never the beach. And I thought about how I wanted to spend the next few years of my life. If someone else could have run Oracle better, I would have been thrilled. I don't feel like I have to be the center of the attention, though if I'm best equipped to do the job, I'm quite willing to make the effort and do the job. If someone else can do the job better, God bless.

Hardware Envy

My heroes include Churchill and MacArthur—people who didn't follow convention. There's an incredible need in all of us to want to belong, and we do a lot of things to join up. When one group wants to show that they're different—maybe everyone's wearing their hair short—everyone in that group wears their hair long. But they're still all conforming with their peers. So we conform in our way of dress, in our way of thinking, and in the way we do business. There's incredible conformity, doing things exactly the way other people do it. That makes us not threatening to the group. Unfortunately, it's very hard to innovate when you're being like everybody else because the group will annihilate you. Winston Churchill was ridiculed and not just by the opposition party—he was ostracized by his own party.

They thought he was a warmonger. He kept wanting England to arm, and he kept saying that this guy Hitler was an enormous danger. At the time, Hitler had a lot of supporters, both in England and in this country. There were all sorts of people in the mid-'30s who thought Hitler was okay. And it was Churchill saying, "Wait a second, this guy's very, very dangerous and very, very bad."

Take someone like MacArthur. Roosevelt would never give MacArthur enough troops or enough planes to really go ahead and attack the Japanese. MacArthur thought it was kind of bad form to lose a lot of soldiers. So MacArthur would simply bypass strong points—go around them. All the young kids who were sent out from West Point to be on his staff thought he was quite literally crazy. They thought his plans were quite, quite strange, and they rejected them. But when his plans kept on yielding one enormous, stunning success after stunning success, they just said, "Okay, whatever—you're amazing. Let's keep doing this."

Steve Jobs says I've got a terrible case of hardware envy because it's tangible. You know, he can bring it home at Thanksgiving and show people, "This is what I make," like the iMac or the Palm Pilot, or something like that. Oracle's products—you can't touch it; I can't hold it up for the camera.

At one time, we almost bought Apple. In fact, if Steve hadn't told me he didn't want us to, we would have. We had all the money lined up: I had Donaldson, Lufkin, and Jenrette underwriting the deal. But Steve didn't want to do it. Apple's the only company, by the way—not true of Dell, not true of IBM—Apple's the only lifestyle brand in the computer industry. Apple is really a unique property in the computer industry. Apple's cool. There are no other cool companies in my industry. None.

And All the Rest

There are probably more pluses than minuses to being well known. But there are some minuses. I love Walter Cronkite. Walter Cronkite's a serious sailor; I'm a serious sailor—I know Walter pretty well. We've had a lot of conversations about the media. I'm also good friends with Ted Turner and Rupert Murdoch. And the news has become the entertainment business, and the personal lives of celebrities are just part of the entertainment. So get used to it if you're a CEO.

Bill Clinton signed on to be president of the United States— the most powerful man in the world. He certainly was the center of a lot of amusement and ridicule in the last few years. Which I think is unfortunate, but it's about ratings, right? They've got a business to run. Television's a business, and they need ratings and they want viewers. If . . . talking about Bill Clinton's sex life or my sex life on television gets more people to watch, that's what they put on. They should at least give me royalties if they're going to use my personal life as entertainment.

I was Bill Clinton's second-largest contributor when he ran for president the first time. When he announced that America's biggest crisis was health care, I was horrified. I thought America's biggest crisis was education.

I saw people from all over the world rushing to the United States for health care. Everyone was coming here to get health care. Now, do we have problems with access for some people to the health care system? Absolutely. So there are definitely problems with our health care system. But is this the biggest crisis facing America? I don't think so.

I didn't see anyone coming from around the world to send their kids to the third grade in public school in the United States. The public schools have monopolies on education, and they are doing a horrifically bad job.

I think school choice is very important. I'm very, very pro-choice. Human beings should get to choose. So I'm a big fan of the charter school systems and a big fan of vouchers.

I am a Democrat, by the way—and while the teachers' unions are incredibly against the voucher system, another one of the anchors of the Democratic party—the African American community—is wildly for vouchers.

We have public colleges and we have private colleges, and the balance has created the best higher education system in the world. We have an absolute monopoly for the public schools in K through 12, and it's created a horrible system. We need to have school choice; we need to go back to neighborhood schools.

I'm very interested in biotechnology. Both my biological mother and my adopted mother died of cancer. I own a biotechnology company in Israel that has just published an extraordinary piece of research in *Science* magazine. Seventy percent of all cancers have damage to a gene called P53. It turns out we have cancers starting in our body all the time, and there's a mechanism inside of all of our cells to detect when the cell is severely damaged and the cell commits suicide. And that suicide mechanism is regulated by this gene, P53. It turns out that cancer goes wild when the P53 gene is damaged in a cell, and it can't commit suicide and becomes cancerous. It starts to duplicate, and tumors form, and they metastasize and all sorts of bad things happen. The paper that we published is a new technique on how to turn off the P53 gene in healthy cells so your good cells don't commit suicide.

I have two children. My son's 16 and an aerobatic pilot. I think he's become an incredibly mature kid as a result of him learning how to fly when he was 13 years old. I think the kids are much more at risk with drugs in school than they are in airplanes. So I actually rest pretty comfortably about him flying. My daughter's 13, and just won the science fair. I think she wants to be a doctor or a veterinarian.

If I was giving them advice, I wouldn't start with talking about being an entrepreneur. I think you've got to figure out what in life makes you happy. You know, both these kids don't have to worry about money and survival day to day. They have a much harder thing to worry about—what it is they really want.

〰

As I write this, today's *San Francisco Chronicle* has, as its cover story, the first look at Larry Ellison's new home in Woodside, California. Half completed, it is estimated to cost $100 million. It has two terraced ponds, several acres each in size, and to create it Ellison ripped out an architectural gem, a Julia Morgan–designed home. As Morgan was also the architect of William Randolph Hearst's San Simeon resort, the act was fraught with symbolism.

Because Woodside, fearful of precisely this kind of excess, has instituted zoning that doesn't allow homes larger than 7,000 square feet, Ellison has built multiple structures slightly smaller than that size, linking them together with walkways and underground tunnels. He has surrounded them with tons of Chinese granite shipped across the Pacific. When it is done, Larry Ellison will be able to land in San Jose in his personal jet, ignoring curfew hours and waking up sleeping workers on the approach path, then race home to his Xanadu. There, in his samurai robes, he can walk about the sculptured gardens and dream of triumphing over his enemies. His fantasy will be complete.

Kim Polese
Cofounder and Chief Strategy Officer, Marimba

The Woman
- Born on November 13, 1961
- Grew up in Berkeley, California
- Earned a B.S. in biophysics from the University of California, Berkeley, and studied computer science at the University of Washington
- Single

The Entrepreneur
- Cofounded Marimba in 1996
- Former product manager at Sun, where she led the development and promotion of Java
- Marimba year 2000 revenues: $44 million (fiscal year ending 12/31/00)

"I know many, many entrepreneurs who do sell out and then instead of feeling happy or fulfilled, they're depressed because they realize that wasn't really what they wanted after all. It's interactions with other people. It's testing yourself. It's challenging yourself. It's creating. It's being in the swim of things. That's what makes life fun. Not cashing out. That's very ephemeral."

Kim Polese's reputation far preceded her—so much that I initially resisted inviting her to the series. Luckily, Bob and Ann talked me into keeping her in the lineup; otherwise, I would have missed a remarkable lesson in courage.

Polese was famous even before she was successful. She had first been noticed in the high-tech world as the demon marketer and missionary for Sun's then-new programming language, Java. So even though it made her one of the Valley's first high-tech CEOs, it was still not a big surprise when she was tapped to head a new software start-up called Marimba.

Marimba had taken off with considerable fanfare, much of it due to the presence of Polese, but then had struggled. Her reputation, for good or bad, had soared much higher. Being a good-looking woman had certainly never been a handicap for her, but now, standing in the public eye, it began to eclipse the rest of Polese's career. High-tech CEOs were middle-aged guys with eyes like raptors, not beautiful young blondes who danced after a long day at the office. It wasn't long before Kim Polese was the pinup girl for a million nerds.

At first Polese went along with it, assuming the celebrity was good for business. It may have been; certainly Marimba got more attention in the early days than it deserved. But personally, it was catastrophic. The low point came when Polese foolishly agreed to pose for a magazine shot in dance leotards that gave her negative publicity and tarnished her reputation for years. As it happened, I wrote a rather scathing comment at this time about Polese as Cat-woman. Furthermore, each morning in the Forbes lobby, I had to walk past a backlit Forbes advertisement featuring a close-up of Kim Polese looking like a thoughtful Dyan Cannon.

So when her name came up as a possible guest on the series, I asked whether she was serious enough to be with such a heavy-weight crowd. My doubts only grew when Polese demanded that we come down to Marimba and meet with her to explain what the show would be about.

The shoot itself began on a note of alarm. Polese arrived puffy-eyed and very quiet, looking much older and sadder than she'd seemed just a few weeks before. The makeup lady took forever try-ing to get her ready for filming, and through it all Kim barely spoke a word.

It was only as I was walking toward the set that I found out why. Her PR person, Susan Woods, took me aside to a dark cor-ner of the studio and whispered to me an explanation. It seemed that in the last two weeks, Polese's mother had been incapaci-tated by a stroke, and her beloved father, probably from the trauma of seeing his wife so ill, had died. Polese had buried him the day before.

"Good Lord," I whispered, looking over at the woman, shrouded in sadness, sitting on the set. "She doesn't have to do this. Does she want to postpone?"

"No," said Woods emphatically. "She says she made you a promise and she intends to go through with it."

It was with a whole different perspective that I interviewed Kim Polese that day. It might have been different had this been a pure business show, where she could have fallen back on financials and growth projections. But this was the most personal type of interview, about her childhood, her dreams, her family. I had to ask Kim about her parents, as they were such a large part of her life. As I did, I could see her steel herself and fight back tears. But, with almost superhuman will, she held herself together—and even used the moment to tell the world with pride about her father.

Before the interview was over, she had become my heroine. And I have admired her ever since.

〰

Immigrant's Daughter

I grew up in Berkeley and I love Berkeley. I think it's the most beautiful place on earth. It's probably where I'll end up eventually.

My parents were European immigrants. They came from the Old World, northern Italy, and there was a real strong work ethic. Sometimes people think since I grew up in Berkeley that I had hippies for parents, but it's quite the contrary.

My dad actually came here to the States in 1911. He came through Ellis Island and settled in Richmond, California, when the Bay Area was just farmland.

He didn't go to college, but he did work in the naval shipyards in Alameda and Hunters Point. His background was in machining, tools, and creation of mechanical objects. In World War II, he was building Liberty ships. He worked his way up through the ranks and became chief planner at Hunters Point, which was a big position there.

After he left the navy, he started his own machine and tool shop in Richmond that he operated well into his 70s. My mother was a homemaker and also worked with my dad in the machine shop, running the back room.

I would go down and help him run the lathe sometimes. It wasn't really my bag, but I actually was fascinated by what he was doing because it was a combination of engineering and art. That's what machine and design really is. What I liked about it was the ability to create any part, both envision it and then actually design and produce it.

Growing up I was sort of a tomboy, riding my bike every day and running track and stuff. In seventh grade I had a best friend who was into dance very seriously and kept encouraging me to try it. I thought it was for sissies, and you'd have to wear pink tutus and stuff.

But once I tried dance, I just loved it, because it was so challenging athletically. It was everything. It was artistic expression. It was music. It was rhythm. It was flexibility.

It's a wonderful balance to work, because I can just completely lose myself. I have to focus on a combination that I'm learning, and the way that I'm interpreting the music. I have to remember the choreography. There's just a lot to it. It's not like being on the Stairmaster and cranking away. I love dance. It's part of who I am.

My parents really instilled in me a very strong work ethic, a sense of responsibility, self-sufficiency, and very high expectations. So those were the things I grew up with, not the free love Berkeley aura.

First of all, in my family, TV was verboten and studying was absolutely expected. Straight A's were expected. There were very, very high expectations from both parents, particularly my dad.

I think it was a desire to have this generation of the family be the first to attend university and realize the American dream.

I'm actually very grateful to my parents for encouraging me. Really not even encouraging me, but expecting me to excel in sciences—in particular, science and engineering was highly respected in my family.

Hitting the Books

Growing up in Berkeley, I always intended to go to the University of California at Berkeley (Cal). I always assumed that I would. I don't know why. It's funny, I didn't even think about applying to other colleges. I only applied to Cal. It's just that it was so much a part of the community, I guess that was what I just assumed I'd do.

I actually went up to the Lawrence Hall of Science (a public science museum for children), which was connected with the university when I was a little kid, and that's when I got really interested and excited about science. I earned a degree in biophysics. It's the study of physical science applied to biological phenomena. An example would be the MRI—magnetic resonance imaging—which is where you're actually studying the physics of organic tissues, but you're using physical sciences to do it.

I just always loved science. I was sort of a geek since I was a little kid. I was considering going into medical school, but biophysics was appealing, because it was actually the broadest array of sciences I could take. It allowed me to take everything from computer science to physics to anatomy. It wasn't an easy major, but actually I loved it.

I wasn't in the sorority scene. I wasn't a big socializer in college. I actually hit the books, but I had fun. I lived at home for much of the time that I went to Cal because we lived pretty close to the university. In retrospect, it probably would have been a good idea to completely uproot myself and go somewhere else.

I took my first computer science class at Cal when I was a junior and it was a turning point for me. After I graduated from Cal, I went up to the University of Washington in Seattle for a year. The reason I went up to UW was that I wanted to get more computer science under my belt because at that point in 1984, I had decided that computer science is really where I wanted to focus.

I loved programming. I just loved it. It's the fact that you have such utter control when you're creating a program. You really are the master of your universe. It was about creating, but it was also science.

Then there was this aspect of having control over this world that you're creating, which is the program. So I just loved it.

I didn't actually enroll in a formal degree program at University of Washington (UW). What I wanted to do was get more computer science under my belt. I had just spent five years at Cal getting a biophysics undergraduate degree, and I wasn't ready to go back for another four years or whatever it would have taken to get a master's in essentially a brand new area.

UW had a postbaccalaureate program where you can take classes and get grades, but you're not actually working formally toward a degree. I just wanted to figure out, "Is this something I wanted to do?" I decided I'd give it a year and see how it felt. I was a serious student; I wasn't much fun.

At the end of that year, I realized I really wanted to start working. I wanted to be in the swim of things. I was kind of tired of going to school. So I came down to the Bay Area and got my first job. Both parents really encouraged me to get out there in the world and follow my own path.

Practical Lessons

I came to Silicon Valley in the beginning of 1985. I was trying to decide really what I wanted to do. I wasn't even sure, frankly, that I would be able to sit still eight hours a day for a regular desk job. I'd never done that before.

I'm a very active person. I was actually debating whether I should become a bicycle messenger, because I found that idea very appealing. I'd probably still be a bicycle messenger if I had done that. But a job offer came through from a company called Intelli-Corp, which was an artificial intelligence software company. We developed expert systems software that helps computers think or act like people in the way that they do reasoning.

I was a technical support engineer. I started out by answering the phones and helping people figure out how to use this $75,000 piece of software. It was a unique technical support experience, though, because it's not like you just flip to the manual and say, "Okay, press the orange button." These were big corporate clients, and this was a very complex system.

It was a very elaborate, expert system, and the company was full of Ph.D.s who designed a very complicated rules system. You had to understand the nuances of this thing.

IntelliCorp was a company of incredibly bright people. It was just like being back at the university, but among the cream of the student crop. I learned some lessons there, because I realized that great technology and brilliant people are not enough. You need a real business application. And reality needs to be tied into all of this fabulous technology.

That was a lesson that certainly wasn't brought home until the company started having trouble. It became clear that the market wasn't quite there and that two and two wasn't adding up when it came to the company's abilities to actually use this technology in the real world.

I was at IntelliCorp for three years and actually ended up doing consulting gigs off site to places like McDonnell Douglas, helping them design systems.

When I left IntelliCorp I felt that I wanted to be part of something larger, and Sun Microsystems (Sun) was a company on the move. The transition for me was, they were starting an artificial intelligence program at Sun.

Sun Rise

In 1989, I think that Sun was about 8,000 people or so when I started. It was big. I ran their support program for AI but realized that it just wasn't challenging. It was just too easy. I didn't feel like I was being stretched or tested.

I found out about a job opening as a product manager of C++, which was a brand new programming language. This was when

Kim Polese with her father. Always Daddy's little girl.

object-oriented programming was very hot and very exciting. The idea of being a product manager was really appealing to me, because it was almost like running your own company in a sense. You had total responsibility for what this product would be, down to the very minute technical features, to the branding and packaging.

This was my first real taste of entrepreneurship, and I just loved it. It was incredibly challenging. It was the kind of job where people burned out. In fact, I was warned, "You're probably not going to last in this job more than a year," because most people don't. It's just very demanding. You don't have people reporting to you, but you have total responsibility for how the product turns out.

In 1993, I found out about this secret project called Green at Sun. I got a demo of the technology and I was just blown away completely. I just was amazed that this technology would exist because it was what programming languages should be.

I was very familiar with programming languages at that time and I realized, "This stuff is going to rock the world when it gets out there, and I want to be part of that." And they were looking for a product manager. I interviewed. The team wanted to hire me. And I came on board.

Sun had created a company called First Person to productize this technology. It was a spin-off company of Sun. At that time, it was aimed toward the interactive television set-top box PDA [personal digital assistant] market. But it became clear pretty quickly that that market wasn't ready yet.

So I cowrote a business plan that recommended taking this technology, putting it on the old desktop PCs and Macintoshes. This technology was later labeled Java.

None of us saw the Internet explosion coming. But one thing was clear: I remember when we were writing this plan in '93, the sale of PCs, Macintoshes, the incredible rate of adoption of AOL and other online services—it was just staggering, the growth rate, the numbers. And that was clearly showing that a trend was ready to explode.

We introduced Java to the world in the spring of '95. This was a last-ditch effort, actually, to get it out there before it got flushed or cancelled. We almost didn't make it. It was throw it over the wall and, hope to God, Sun lets us put it out there and hope that people understand the potential of this technology. It was frustrating, but we persevered.

I wasn't thinking about my career at that time. I would kill myself trying to do my part to get this technology out to the world, because I knew how important it was from a pure technology standpoint.

I think it's just part of my makeup. I'm just extremely driven, and once I get my teeth in something, I just don't give up.

My parents are certainly that way. They're very much self-sufficient and extremely driven and very results-oriented. It's not so much for the achievement or the degree or the notoriety. It's for getting a job done, and being proud of that, creating something and seeing it to the end, seeing it through. You have to do it all. You finish the process. You give it your all.

We announced Java in March of '95, gave our first newspaper interview, and the thing just took off. It completely blew us away. We had no idea. I remember the day after I gave that interview to this reporter from the *San Jose Mercury News*, I flipped to the business section to see if there was a little item about it. It wasn't in there, and I was just really disappointed: "I guess he didn't get it." Then I flipped over to the front page of the paper, and it was above the fold. It was the headline of the paper that day, "Why Sun Thinks Hot Java Will Give You A Lift." And he got it, clearly. And the phones started ringing that day. It was the 23rd of March, '95, and it never stopped. And my life really changed fundamentally in a big way.

I was just so pleased that the right thing happened for once, because there's so many technologies you work on that never see the light of day because of stupid business decisions or policies.

The notoriety I received was just a complete and total shock. But I was the product manager, and so I was the visible spokesperson evangelizing Java and explaining to the rest of Sun and the world what it meant.

It was part of my job. I was [so] thrilled that we had gotten this thing out there that I was just pleased as punch to step up and talk about it.

It was very strange for me, because I am not someone who sought the limelight. I didn't go out there trying to promote myself or get my time in front of the camera. I had not really been in the papers before.

There was this fascination with the oddity of having a young woman evangelizing a very technical product. It was just unusual, and the media picked up on that. Anytime there's something that's different, it instantly gets blown out of proportion. I thought it was just very silly and distracting, but I didn't let it distract me from what I was doing. On the one hand, I had perspective, but I was disappointed on behalf of my coworkers.

Independence

I never ran a business as a kid other than just lemonade stands and the standard stuff, but I always had a deep-down desire to be an entrepreneur—to have my own business. I didn't know what it would be or when it would be, but I knew it would—at a certain point—become clear to me.

The motive was to be independent. It was to run my own show. It was to create something.

First Person had been like a start-up company. It had actually been a separate company, only about, you know, 35, 40 of us off site. It had not been like working for a big company. So for the last three years, I had really worked at a start-up company. Although it was funded by Sun, it was a start-up company. We had been in complete control of our destiny. And I had been able to create this whole marketing program around Java.

I realized that all of Sun was descending on Java, and Java was becoming Sun. I would never have the kind of control and ability to chart my own destiny and get what I wanted done with a big company becoming part of the whole scene again.

I started talking to three other coworkers on the Java team, and we all started talking at the same time—"You know, we should really go and start a company." We knew people were going to start companies based on Java and all these great Web technologies, and we thought we should be one of those guys. If we're ever going to do it, now's the time.

My dad lived through the Depression and came from an era where you work for a company for 40 years. You have your retirement fund that you build up and all of that. So he was worried about what I was planning to go and do. But at the end of the day, he really encouraged me to do it, because he understood that entrepreneurial drive. He had it himself. And I think he knew that I needed to give this a shot. So he supported me. He was worried. He still didn't quite understand why I would be walking away from this 40-year career. But you know, he was supportive.

When we started the company, we decided to not engage the venture capitalists for the first half year. We wanted to be in control again of our own destiny and we wanted to build value into the company before we started giving pieces of it away.

We each contributed $15,000 to buy machines and software and rent space. We actually worked in a defunct storage space of a stationery store in downtown Palo Alto. It was a pretty funky space and we didn't take any salaries, but we held off on VC money.

We wanted the discipline, really, of driving ourselves. We wanted to prove it to ourselves that we had what it took. We knew we could raise $5 million at the drop of a hat. But you get sort of fat and lazy and unfocused if you don't have a plan already in mind, and if you don't have something that really is driving you. Not being paid and having the uncertainty of having no safety net is a great motivator.

Tango

When we started Marimba, we got more attention than most start-ups ever get. I started getting all of this personal attention and all this "Madonna of Silicon Valley" sexual stuff. It detracted from what I was saying. I would be giving interviews, and instead of the interview reflecting what I was saying, it would end up being about what I was wearing or who I had dinner with last night or some ridiculous thing. That was really a disservice to my cofounders and to the people that I was building this great company with, because it took attention away from what was important. So that was the frustration for me.

But it was a two-edged sword. I hate this silly attention I'm getting but on the other hand, this is good PR for a little start-up. I basically had to walk the line. As a CEO of a new start-up company, if *Business Week* or some publication such as that calls me and wants to interview me about the company, I should be shot if I said no. But then the rub is, how am I ultimately portrayed, and how is the company portrayed in the piece? So it definitely was a conflict. Ultimately it turned out to be, I think, a benefit.

Naming the company was fun. I like names that are easy to remember and spell and pronounce, and, more importantly, reflect the energy or the personality of the company or the product. And so Marimba, to me, made a lot of sense, because all of us are either musicians, or I'm a dancer, and there's a spirit and energy to the company that I wanted to have reflected in the name.

I never liked nerdy names, because they are forgettable. And I felt that in the case of Java, this was an unforgettable technology, and it should have a name that reflected that. The same was true with the company that we were building, Marimba.

I think of IPO [initial public offering] day as an important event in time in the process of building a great company. It was actually a wonderful day. I remember the night before: "Yeah, you know, we're going public tomorrow."

Thinking I was going to be really, really rich was the last thing on my mind. Believe it or not, what I really cared about, and what my cofounders cared about, was building a great company. The wealth was on paper, and it doesn't become real until you actually build the company that builds in the value that it's speculating in the market.

I was concerned that our employees might get distracted by the IPO and the money, because I had other CEOs of companies telling me that that's the classic syndrome. So for the almost-year prior—a good six, eight months prior to the event itself—I would talk to the company about that. I hold monthly, what I call, "all hands meetings"—the whole company gathers, and that's something we talked about.

And I would talk also one on one with people about it, and really tried to drive home that what we're doing here, this is just an event in time. And this is not the end. This is really the beginning of building a great company. It's very difficult in this environment we're in in Silicon Valley today for people to remain focused on that.

The Great Dance

I'm having more fun than ever. More than in a start-up, because every phase is a new challenge. It evolves and changes, and that makes it more exciting and fascinating.

It's easy to start a company, and relatively easy to even take one public these days, sadly enough. But the challenge is building a great public company. Very few companies do that, and I love a challenge. So that, to me, is the thing that I'm working on now with the rest of the company.

We're still an early-stage company. I think people these days have this impression that you're done when you're IPO, and then it's time to go on to the next. That's the wrong mind-set, and I am trying to make sure that the people in the company understand that that's not the end goal. That it's really the beginning of what the exciting challenge is.

What you have to do is constantly be smarter than the next guy out there, and be surveying the landscape and be listening to your customers and seeing the trends that are emerging, and putting the pieces together. And you can't ever stop doing that. You have to constantly be vigilant about doing that. There's no rest, and that's what's so fun about it. It's this endless challenge.

I don't think you build a successful company, no matter what, if you have the intention of selling it off. My philosophy is, no matter what you ultimately do, you have to have your sights set high and you have to be looking out in the future, because then you build a company that is attractive, whether it's to the public market or to a potential acquirer.

I think the challenge and the really exciting part of all of this is building a real company. I get turned off by the mentality that I think is increasing in the Valley, which is to cash out. You know, start a company, and as you're starting it, the exit strategy is the important thing you're deciding.

I find that to be very sad, because what made this Valley great, this industry great, was people like Hewlett and Packard, Andy Grove, Scott McNealy, and others who were really focused on building a great company for the challenge of doing that, and for the thrill of creating something solid.

I worry about the Valley and the industry losing what made it great—the emphasis on innovation, creating something, and building a success over the long term. That doesn't happen overnight, and I think there's almost a disease that's starting to creep into the Valley, into the industry today.

I don't want to cast aspersions on people who create a great product and then sell their company, because there's nothing wrong with selling your company.

It happens more often than not. It's very rare that you see an Intel or a Cisco or Sun—founders that go all the way with a company, and build it into literally a billion dollars in revenues—not market cap. But I think it's important for young entrepreneurs in this Valley to still have something to aspire to that has value. There is today too much emphasis on cashing out.

There really are young people today who are 25 who are only worth—"only worth"—$20 million, who think they're just an utter failure, and they're depressed about it. And it's just sick.

I would tell them that one of life's greatest joys is working together with a team and creating something. And all being committed to doing that over a series of months and years. It doesn't happen overnight if you're creating something real. That is one of the great joys of not only this industry, but life. And that if you get a shot at doing that, you should give it your all.

That means ultimately building a real company. Not going for the money, not cashing out, but building something real. I think people forget the fact that this is a life experience. This is part of life. This is not just about making money.

After the interview was completed, Kim Polese's career took some remarkable turns. Marimba, after struggling for a couple years, began to turn itself around. It even went public, finally making Polese as successful as she was famous.

Then, in July 2000, Kim Polese did a most extraordinary thing: She stepped down as CEO to be the chief strategy officer and retained her position as chairman of the board. It was a smart move, but almost unprecedented by someone so young. Most CEO/entrepreneurs have to be dragged out of their CEO position. Kim made up her mind and did it. It was an act of enormous will.

Photo by John Harding

T.J. Rodgers
Founder, CEO, President, and Director, Cypress Semiconductor

The Man
- Born on March 15, 1948
- Earned a B.A. in physics and chemistry at Dartmouth College and a master's and Ph.D. in electrical engineering at Stanford
- Single

The Entrepreneur
- Founded Cypress Semiconductor in 1982 and built it into a leading international supplier of integrated circuits
- Cypress year 2000 revenues: $1.3 billion (fiscal year ending 12/31/00)

"We've had two recessions in seventeen years, and each was one year long and each was painful. But I'm glad I had those for training. They were tough times, but I think I'm a better manager for it."

$\mathcal{M}$y first introduction to T.J. Rodgers was almost 15 years ago, during the inaugural of my first public television series, *Malone*. The biggest U.S. semiconductor companies, led by the sainted Bob Noyce of Intel Corporation, had talked the federal government into putting up $250 million for a research facility, Sematech, to improve chip manufacturing processes.

As a lifelong libertarian, as well as the CEO of a small semiconductor company that had not been allowed to participate, Rodgers came on my show to denounce Sematech, in the harshest of terms. You might as well take the money and burn it on the White House lawn, he declared, or better yet: Divide it into 250 million-dollar chunks and give them to entrepreneurs to start new companies. History proved Rodgers right.

The next time we shared a stage, it was in front of thousands at the first meeting of Joint Venture Silicon Valley, an attempt to bring the Valley's business, government, and educational leaders together in a common cause. My job was to introduce Rodgers. I warned people in the audience to brace themselves. Rodgers then leaped onto the stage and proceeded—in the name of unity, of course—to publicly eviscerate the San Jose city government. A few minutes later I found myself in a side room being screamed at by the mayor's chief of staff.

One of the photos Rodgers sent us to use with the TV series was a full frontal picture of him, stark naked, at age two. To me, that photo says everything about T.J. Rodgers: He is fearless, absolutely straightforward, and not without a sense of humor. Rodgers is honest with his customers, absolutely loyal to his employees, and a junkyard dog with his enemies. The list of the last group includes Jesse Jackson, whom he called a race hustler; a nun, whom he told to stay out of Cypress Semiconductor's business; and statists of every stripe. He announces these views in venues as diverse as the *Wall Street Journal* and local television, and even in white papers he pens and then makes available to anyone interested.

Watching him build, through good times and bad, Cypress Semi from nothing into a billion-dollar corporation has been one of the most fascinating stories in Silicon Valley history. At times it seemed as though the only thing holding the company together was Rodgers's will to win. And woe to anyone who threatens his company: When Texas Instruments, a few years back, tried to use its old patents to leverage money out of its competitors, the company made the mistake of calling Cypress. Rodgers told TI to go to hell. Go ahead and sue me, he told that company's lawyers, and I'll fight you to the death. He has never, ever settled a case against Cypress—in fact, he keeps a wall covered with copies of complaints filed against the company.

Interviewing T.J. Rodgers is always an unforgettable experience. After all these years, he can still catch me unguarded with a remark that is so impolitic or outrageous or politically incorrect that I literally sputter for a few seconds, trying to come up with a rejoinder. And every time, I see him break into the "gotcha" grin of a mischievous five-year-old.

≋

A Born Entrepreneur

I grew up in Oshkosh, Wisconsin. My dad was a used-car salesman and my mother was a fifth-grade teacher. I've always been an entrepreneur. My mother likes to tell a story about how she, for a reward one time, gave me a half a watermelon and then found me selling it out in front of the house—I was making money on it.

My parents met during World War II. My mother was actually sent and became an instructor in electronics, a woman instructor in radio electronics, or WIRE. There were WACs and WIREs.

My dad was a pilot. He flew DC-3s with troops and supplies in the Southwest Pacific for MacArthur's forces. They fell in love. She was educated and became a teacher, and he wasn't, and selling cars was what he could do. But he's a real solid person whom people trust, and he's built a good client list and made a good living at it.

My mother was a driving force for education in our house. It was ordained that I was going to go to college, no matter what. Anything less than a Ph.D. would have been failure.

I played guard on the Dartmouth football team. I weighed, at that time, about 195 pounds, and I was pretty fast. So in the Ivy League, which you know isn't pro like the other schools are, you could easily play football at 195 pounds.

I was quite competitive. I remember one day we played Holy Cross. They had a center who was kind of a wiry, gawky kid. He wasn't bigger, but he was taller than me. I've never played against a more frustrating person. Anytime he wanted me to move in some direction, that's where I ended up. I never got past him. I never made a tackle. I never got to the quarterback, and it was all day long. He completely controlled me. I came off the field and I thought the coach was going to chew me out. Instead, the coach slapped me on the back and said, "That kid could play on anybody's team." I never found out his name.

I was a good student at Oshkosh High School, but it was Oshkosh High School. When I hit the big leagues, all of a sudden the other students were from Exeter and Andover and they were very, very good. I never had failed at anything, and I wasn't about not to be a very top student at Dartmouth. So I studied my butt off for four years. I gave up football after a year. I took on a second major, physics and chemistry. I just wouldn't do anything but academics.

My mother is the person that got me involved in electronics. In World War II, she got her degree in elementary education, then, in order to get a date with a "cute" young lieutenant in the lobby, she took the entry test into the United States Army Air Force. She didn't get a tumble from the lieutenant, but she did get accepted into the Air Force. They tested her and they sent her to St. Louis University and she got a master's degree in radio electronics. She taught that during World War II. So she's still got books about electronics at home.

I've actually used one of her books in a trial. Texas Instruments was suing us about a circuit that had been around forever. But the circuit, having been reinvented for the 540th time, was now a programmable logic device.

We had picked two women, one of whom we thought would be the foreperson, to sit on the jury. On the stand, I made the comment that the circuit wasn't new, that it existed in the vacuum tube form during World War II. And, of course, the other lawyer couldn't resist having that bait thrown in front of him, so he asked me when I was born and I said 1948.

He said, "Well, how would you know anything about World War II electronics?" Then I got to tell him about my mother teaching in the Army. And, of course, these women are sitting in the jury. That *Texas* jury wiped out the case and patent in 20 minutes.

In high school I was interested in chemistry, and I got to Dartmouth and I liked it but started losing steam. I started in chemistry, got tired of it, and I finished as a physics major. I graduated with both majors from Dartmouth.

I was accepted all over to grad school, but I was so tired of Wisconsin and New Hampshire winters that I picked California. I was accepted into the department of electrical engineering at Stanford, so I put my stuff in a U-Haul and, first time west of the Mississippi, I drove to California, where it was warm.

I found out when I got there that all the students at Stanford wanted to start a company, and I liked that. We would spend our lunchtimes talking about what ideas we have that we can commercialize.

I even got in a conflict with Stanford, where I was inventing things at Stanford specifically to start a company. The school started pressing me to sign away my patent rights to them. I wouldn't knuckle under. So I went out and found a fellowship that actually left you with your patent rights. I flipped it around and said to the school, "I'm paying full tuition, would you like me as a student? And, by the way, I own my patent rights and I'm not going to give them to you." I patented a couple of inventions at Stanford.

A Perverse Personality

The last few years have been character-building years. It's a different paradigm for management. You're managing to try to return to profitability. The way I always work is that you do the best job you can do. You convince yourself that you're managing competently and you go home and let it slide. You just can't get hung up on it; otherwise, it devastates you.

I have kind of a perverse personality, where I feel like I can contribute more in tough times. I've been around now at Cypress for 18 years, and people know that I'm in for the long haul. I can add stability. During the rah-rah times anybody can run a company. Anybody can hire more people, give them more money.

Handling the pressures personally, I do running, I do movies, and I make wine. Those are what I do. And cook. That's it. So I'm either doing chips or those other four things.

Photo by Lois L. Rodgers

Choirboy: A side of T.J. Rodgers that business competitors and Jesse Jackson have never seen.

The Big Bluff

When I started Cypress, I was sitting in my office at AMD one day and I get a call from a venture capitalist in New York. He was about to fund someone who worked for someone who worked for me. This person was okay, but not great and had an idea for a company that was not even okay.

I didn't want to trash the person, but I said, "Yes, they're capable of doing that." I didn't say he's a great guy and the company idea is great, I just said, yes, the person you're calling about can do what the charter of the company is.

Then I said to the VC, "By the way, if you're giving away money, you ought to fund my company because I've got a lot better idea and I sure can run a company better than the people you're talking about."

I didn't completely have an idea at that time. But he said great, and I went to see him the next week to explain an idea about starting another chip company. After the meeting, the guy said to me, "You've got to see my big-league friend, Ben Rosen," the recent chairman of Compaq. So I flew to Dallas and on that flight from New York to Dallas I did my business plan in pencil, seven pages long. I had in my head the parameters for a chip I was thinking about building and why it would be devastating in the marketplace. Then I extrapolated other equivalent possibilities, added them together, and came up with a crude profit-and-loss statement. And that was good enough. Rosen gave me $7.5 million. That was back in the days when you could start a chip company.

Bad Boy

I got put on the cover of *Business Week*, called "The Bad Boy of Silicon Valley." I'm really happy I have that position. If "bad boy" means a champion of capitalism and a champion of freedom, someone who will not compromise his position, then I can do that forever because I'm wired that way.

Corporate welfare is bad. I said it 10 years before anybody else woke up about it. I was alone when all the welfare grabbers in the semiconductor industry had their palms stuck out to Washington.

I said that Sematech wouldn't help the semiconductor industry that much, and it's true. And I said that we had not lost to the Japanese, which everybody was claiming, and that it would only be a matter of time before we fixed our manufacturing problems, and our inventiveness and our new ideas would overwhelm the Japanese—which was also true.

First of all, I'm a libertarian. There's some parts of what conservatives like that I like. For example, small government and low taxes. There's some parts of what conservatives like such as regulating your sex life and what you snort or drink, which I don't like. With regard to liberals, I share some common ground with them. They're socially libertarian, be who you want to be, do what you want to do, and I believe in that. I just don't like it when they try to take over your money in the form of high taxes and say, "I've got a better idea of what to do with your money than you do."

I'm accused of being political. I'm not. I would never run for office. I wouldn't want to be a senator and I wouldn't want to be the president of the United States. I have a real job. I don't depend on confiscating money from people in order to support myself. I make money for myself and the people that work at Cypress and our shareholders. So I'm a creator of wealth, not a taker of wealth. And I'm political only in the sense that I believe in freedom, I believe in the Constitution and the Declaration of Independence, and I think a lot of entrepreneurs in Silicon Valley haven't got a clue what that means. They don't understand that capitalism—free markets—free minds and free markets—is exactly what allowed them to become rich with their skills. And then they support things that undermine the basic values and the basic economic system that makes Silicon Valley what it is, and that's capitalism.

Jesse and the Sister

I never use an opportunity for PR if I don't truly and deeply believe in the issue. And the issue is very important.

A nun in Pennsylvania writes me a letter that she's going to withhold 13,400 votes from me to be on the board of directors of my own company because, according to her, even though there are no pictures in our annual report, she's decided our board is too white male. A prudent thing might be to ignore her. But the fact is, if you have my job, you have dozens of meddlers who are trying to make you do things that aren't consistent with making your company successful. You've got the nuns who want your board of directors to have a certain demography. You've got the California Retirement Board saying you ought to run your company another way. You've got various government agencies. At the end of the day, one of the things that makes Silicon Valley successful is, companies think just about wanting to succeed: I'm not going to break any laws, but I'm going to make a new workstation, some new software, a new Java.

Cypress is a company and it's owned by shareholders. So my first priority is to look after my shareholders' interests. Period. The reason I publicly challenged her was, she's a classic example of someone who nominally stands for good, but in my opinion stands for evil. She's doing bad, messing up the economy that supports a lot of people, for what she perceives to be good. And therefore she was an ideal person to make that statement about.

I've received a thousand letters based on my exchange with her. Ten times more letters than I ever received on any other thing I've ever written. And they were 91 percent favorable and 9 percent unfavorable. It was overwhelming. It's the most overwhelmingly favorable thing I've ever written. Everybody else saw her as an authoritarian who had a certain set of beliefs, which were beliefs that she couldn't justify. But being a nun, she lives in a world of having beliefs she doesn't need to justify, she just believes because it is, and she was trying to jam those beliefs down my throat and my shareholders' throats. I said, the heck with you, we're going to run this company ethically and profitably for our shareholders, not for what you declare is right.

Jesse Jackson came into town and I knew he was going to say a bunch of stuff that would be antagonistic to business. But the return on investment for your shareholders of you making that point is small because he really doesn't matter with regard to your business. You just get a black eye for dealing with the guy.

So I decided to let this one pass. For four days, I absolutely refused to talk to the media. I got all kinds of phone calls because I'm the guy that's willing to speak his mind. But I just didn't want to comment on it. Then I came into work one day and I heard him talking on the radio, and I heard him undermining our values. Undermining freedom. "You will do the following because I'm Jesse and I say." Undermining economic freedom, "You will hire the following people according to quotas because I'm Jesse and I say." And then impugning us.

Cypress has 35 percent minority employment. I don't need a lesson from him about hiring people of all races, colors, and creeds. It's ridiculous. He implied that there's some sort of structural prejudice in me—not me personally, but me slash CEO and in Silicon Valley. I said, I'm not going to let him get away with that. I had my staff call up television reporters to see if they want to talk to me. They showed up and I gave a sort of an intellectual pitch to the first one and then I thought, yep, when that one gets chopped up for the 10 o'clock news, there'll be nothing left. I did the same for the second one, and I thought for the third one: I need to engage here, I need to think of something that's more provocative. So I got up and stuck the microphone in my face and said, "He reminds me of a seagull—he flies into town and craps all over everything and flies out." The reporter was sitting there looking at me like, "Did this guy really say that on tape?"

I understand there was a big debate at the station. It turns out his boss said "You can't show it," and his boss's boss said, "He said it, it's not profane, it's his opinion, he's willing to take responsibility for it, put it on the air." That triggered the *San Jose Mercury News* to ask for dueling editorials.

I'm not into race stuff in the same way I'm not into politics. I'm not into race merchants, which is how Jackson makes his living, by stirring up racial stuff and working his network to make money on that angle. I'm not interested in it because we hire everybody who's talented, whatever color they are, and anybody who walks through Cypress would understand that. But the fact that he was going to start buying shares and making some mandates to companies—I saw him as another nun coming in with the aura of a minister and therefore automatically a good person. I started reading about the guy and the guy's a con man. He has a terrible track record. If you just read what the man says in his web site, it's terrible. If we followed what that man said, Silicon Valley wouldn't exist, literally. In Silicon Valley we have a meritocracy. The reason I have 35 percent minority employees is that of, let's say, 100 of the people who walk in the door, 35 percent are real good and I want to hire them, give them money and stock, and [they] happen to be minorities. So that's the way it works out.

The fact is, once you read about the man, you understand he's a bully, and every bully is a coward. You understand that he has no rational basis to stand on. What he does is pure name-calling. "You're a CEO and therefore you're prejudiced" is every bit as bigoted as he would claim someone is who wouldn't hire somebody for racial reasons. Once I read about him, I realized he was going to be an easy target. He was going to be a balloon that would pop. I realized that no one could like a man like this and he must be deeply resented broadly even in a very liberal area like Silicon Valley.

We don't need people flying in telling us how to run race relations in Silicon Valley. We have a very diverse society, and we just don't need any help—especially from people who make a living doing that kind of stuff.

The fact is, I never consulted with the board about engaging in these debates. If the board wants me running the company, then they get the package. I never asked them what I could publish. I'm an American, I have the right of free speech. If they like me, the package, plus what I say, great. If not, they can find another guy to run the company.

Valley Gestalt

One of the things I'm most proud of is that I have taken the trouble to study and understand what it is that makes us special and different. It's not Java code or biotechnology—those are the things certain companies or industries happen to work on here in Silicon Valley. What makes us special and different here in Silicon Valley is that we're truly capitalists. We invest. There is no safety net. You can go out of business. You can crash into the wall. There are companies, you can count them on both fingers every day, that go out of business, and that's life.

The fact is, by allowing people to take their chance to be a millionaire and fail, and take their chance again and maybe succeed, we've created this incredibly rich society that produces things for everybody in the world, not just to make ourselves rich. I understand that. And I understand why Jesse Jackson or nuns or liberal CEOs who think they're doing good and they really aren't, who undermine that, aren't good. And I'm willing to say it. Right now, the idea that got born in an airplane and typed on a personal computer that I bought with a loan is today worth about $3 billion. That's the market cap at Cypress and I own 2 percent of Cypress, so I ride along with it.

I dislike greatly the resenters of wealth and the haters of freedom who criticize the e-com boys. I don't particularly admire a guy who says, "I'm worth $80 million and I don't wear socks to work." But on the other hand, people gave him the money, so he must have created some value.

What's happening is the American financial system is directing wealth toward where it thinks the world's going to move. We're moving at light speed relative to the Japanese, who probably still have a committee working on the problem, and the Europeans, who are trying to work it out politically. So let the e-millionaires be e-millionaires.

If these people change the world and make us all richer and better off and everybody's standard of living rises because of them, let them have their money. I don't resent people making money, ever—if it's freely given to them and it's not extorted by some sort of government action.

I disagree that the whole character of the Valley's changed and the quick buck is all we're after. I've seen a lot of editorials like that, and I think that has to do partly with [the fact that] people resent quick wealth happening because people have a large contribution to make and get paid for it. As far as changing our use, I didn't go to the drugstore last Saturday because I ordered my stuff from drug-store.com and it showed up in the mail and I saved myself a half an hour out of my life. What's that worth?

The number one advice I'd give them is to work in the best interest of their shareholders for the long term. In other words, don't work to make earnings per share greater this quarter if it means shafting your employees or screwing your customers or pro-ducing crappy quality. If your goal is to be around many years from now, then making money is equivalent to doing right by everybody around you, because you'll be all alone quickly if you don't. As long as they work toward that end, creating wealth for themselves their shareholders, their customers, and the communities in which they live, I can't knock 'em.

Now, on the other hand, could I bring in one of them and put him into a three-year recession in the silicon company and would he be around at the end? Probably not. Do I take pride in that fact? Sure, I do. But just because they don't want to put on pads and smack heads with me doesn't mean that they don't add value and aren't worth the money they're making.

≋

We taped T.J. Rodgers late in the afternoon at the KTEH studios in San Jose. As it happened, it was pledge night. So almost from the moment we finished talking, we had to clear out of the studio.

So Rodgers, Bob Grove, and I retreated to the cafeteria, where we found ourselves in a crowd of nervous phone volunteers from a local Dr. Who fan club. Unlike the entrepreneurs in the series, Rodgers seemed in no hurry to get to his next appointment. And so, standing there, in our makeup and pin-striped suits, amid a gaggle of dancing and giggling Whoeys, the three of us gobbled snacks and drank fruit punch. We talked about the state of the industry, about other guests on the series, and about Rodgers's latest political crusade. But, most of all, we talked about Rodgers's vineyard, where he has committed himself to growing the world's greatest zinfandel. The odds, of course, are against him — which is why he will probably succeed. Finally, after nearly an hour, almost reluctantly, T.J. Rodgers headed off into the night. The room instantly grew smaller without him.

Tom Siebel
Founder, Chairman, and CEO, Siebel Systems

The Man
- Born on November 20, 1952
- Grew up in Wilmette, a suburb of Chicago
- Earned a B.A. in history, and an M.B.A. and M.A. in computer science from the University of Illinois
- Married, four children

The Entrepreneur
- Founded Siebel Systems in 1993 and built it into a successful market leader in enterprise automation software
- Siebel year 2000 revenues: $1.8 billion (fiscal year ending 12/31/00)

"If you look at the real, real core of many of these success stories it's not great visionaries, it's not great entrepreneurs, it's not makers of insanely great technology, it's pretty bright people who came from Baltimore and Chicago and Springfield . . . wherever, who found themselves in the right place at the right time and managed not to foul up the opportunity."

I didn't want to interview Thomas Siebel for this series, but Bob and Ann talked me into it.

It wasn't as if Siebel was undeserving. On the contrary, he is arguably the single most successful entrepreneur in the world over the past five years. The problem was, I was a little too connected to Siebel.

In 1995 I got a call from Tom, whom I barely knew as a former sales executive of Oracle. Siebel had left that company after playing a pivotal role in its success, and then took over Gain Technology. Within a year, in one of the smartest plays Silicon Valley had seen in a long time, Siebel turned around and sold Gain Technology to Oracle's competitor Sybase for about $107 million.

After that shrewd maneuver, one might have predicted that Siebel would walk away from the corporate world to enjoy tycoonship at a very young age. That wasn't the man I met. He was wearing an expensive suit but sitting at a folding card table in a small, rented office near the next office, in an equally spartan setting, where Pat House, his business partner, sat. There were two other employees, including the receptionist/office manager/executive secretary, who had on her desk the one luxury in the place: a jar of M&M's.

Over the past 20 years, I have been approached dozens of times by businessmen who want to write a book with me. Most of them meet me in elegant executive offices or fancy restaurants. And I always tell them no. I had planned to do the same with Tom Siebel. What I hadn't planned on was an encounter with one of the great salesmen of our generation. When I walked out an hour later, I had agreed to coauthor the book (it would be called *Virtual Selling*). What's more, I had agreed to take my half of the advance and royalties in Siebel Systems stock.

How had Tom convinced me? I'm still not sure. There was nothing salesman-like in his manner. He was neither slick nor clever. On the contrary, he seemed the very antithesis of a classic supersalesman. But what he had was pure will, an attitude that said that the deal was already done and that he was merely waiting for me to realize it. He sold me, just as he soon would sell most of the top CEOs of the world on Siebel software.

We wrote the book, usually on the run—once even outlining a chapter while racing down the highway between appointments. All the while, Tom and Pat were building the company from scratch. Literally. They took no venture capital money, instead funding the firm with private investors and the sweat equity of employees and contractors (including me).

The finished book did a lot to enhance Tom's prestige as a knowledge leader in his field. As for me, it was a minor success. On the other hand, my decision to take stock in lieu of cash may have been the luckiest of my life. That's because Siebel Systems, under Tom's leadership, became one of the most successful and fastest-growing companies of the past quarter century, reaching revenues of more than $200 million in just four years. The stock did even better, not only amply rewarding the investors, but making mil-

lionaires of scores of hardworking employees. Tom Siebel, the man
at the folding table, was now a multibillionaire, one of the most
celebrated entrepreneurs of the age.

Thus, my dilemma. How could I interview a man who had been
that important to my bank account? Yet how could I not? I was more
than prepared to ask Siebel tough personal questions—frankly, as a
reporter, I looked forward to it. But it was also crucial that I acknowledge in the show—and as I am doing in this book—the considerable
conflict of interest raised by my interviewing Tom Siebel.

As for the interview itself, I'll leave it to you to judge the results.
These are not the words of a successful entrepreneur enjoying the
fruits of his success, but of a tough, wary, plainspoken CEO who
knows that employees, shareholders, and customers will be watching. Despite that, there are stunning moments, such as when he
speaks about Oracle and Larry Ellison. Then, Tom steps out from
behind the title and delivers opinions that are both heartfelt and
devastating.

I grew up on the North Shore of Chicago, a town called Wilmette,
Illinois. It was a suburban town north of Chicago, a bedroom community, reasonably upscale, close to Lake Michigan, and I think it
was a great place to grow up. At school I played hockey and I wres-
tled. I forget what weight, honestly, but I wasn't very big in high
school and I'm not very big now. Later on, in college, I was
involved in martial arts a little bit.

I'm the sixth of seven children in our family, so it was a zoo at
our house. My mother was a housewife and my father was a promi-
nent and, I think, successful attorney, primarily in business law in
Chicago. The law was in my family. My grandfather was an attorney, my father was an attorney, my eldest brother was an attorney,
and I don't know why I didn't go into law. I was very interested in

ideas related to engineering, science, and medicine, and how the way we think about these problems evolved over the centuries.

We had little businesses as kids. When I was in high school, I cut logs for a living, and then during summers in college we had a painting business and we would paint houses. That's how we made a little money to keep going. I can't say I have any dramatic stories like Michael Dell, where I started at the age of 15 and dropped out by 18 and the rest is history, but I think I exhibited some entrepreneurial tendencies on a very low level.

I attended the University of Illinois at Champaign-Urbana for a long time and received three degrees. One in history, one in business, and one in computer science.

I went to school to learn fundamental skills: how to read, how to write, how to communicate. I was very interested in history and I studied the history of ideas, the history of science, the history of philosophy. I learned a great deal studying these things that affected the way I have behaved in recent years and the way I behave today professionally. That was a very, very valuable background.

I was working very, very hard at that time at college and I did two master's degrees at the same time. I did a four-year program in three years between the two schools, and I had to work pretty hard. So I was really focused on academics.

When I went to graduate school I became interested in information technology and the way I thought information technology might change the world.

I would say my career was affected very much by a sociologist from Harvard by the name of Daniel Bell. Dan Bell wrote an article that was republished by the MIT press in the late '70s, in which he put forth this idea of the postindustrial society. This was a pretty prescient article. He hypothesized that we were about to undergo a change in the underlying structure of the economy on the order of the industrial revolution. Now this is all very common and we read about it every day, but back then it was pretty leading-edge stuff and I was very, very affected by this article.

After undergraduate school, I went into the book publishing business for some years, doing marketing. It was a very small publishing house in rural Illinois, and we did everything from copyediting to writing jacket copy to going to trade shows and representing the company.

In book publishing, we were essentially applying fourteenth-century technology, the Gutenberg press, to deliver information, to entertain, and to persuade. I thought this whole postindustrial society thing, with these new information technologies, was going to replace this. I wanted to be a part of this change that I thought was taking place. I wanted to first develop some expertise in the area, and that's what the University of Illinois graduate school was about. I spent some years getting an advanced degree in information technology and computer science so that I could be familiar with the technologies that would become the currency of the day.

The Oracle Years

After I completed graduate school, business school, and the engineering college, I interviewed with a number of companies. It was the usual suspects. IBM was a very large recruiter at that time.

Then I got a note one day from some company that I had never heard of—nobody had ever heard of at that time—called Oracle Corporation. Oracle had about 40 employees. And they wanted me to come in and be with them. So I went to work for Oracle in Chicago. Then I went to Oracle in Washington, D.C., and it wasn't until a couple of years later, in 1995, that I moved out to headquarters in Silicon Valley.

My early days at Oracle were very exciting times. Oracle grew over 100 percent a year for 11 years, and that was pretty rapid growth in those days. One hundred percent growth a year set big numbers in the early '80s. Now it's not so big, but those were big numbers and it was really the professional experience of a lifetime. The average age at Oracle might have been 23 or 24 years old.

There were a bunch of young, bright, enthusiastic people who were out to change the world and they were on something of a mission and it was a great place to work.

When I left in 1990, I think it was a $900 million company and had about 12,000 employees, if I'm not mistaken. I was the group vice president for Oracle USA. I was responsible for marketing worldwide, I was responsible for all the alliances, all the OEMs [original equipment manufacturers], all the VAR [value-added resellers] relationships and direct marketing: telesales, telemarketing, these aspects of the business.

I think that Oracle, in 1990, was running out of management. The infrastructure was not there; the systems were not there. The place was clearly out of control. This is when they were just about to hit the wall. It was an incredibly aggressive place. The philosophy was very much about winning at all costs.

If you looked at the management team that they had in place at Oracle at that time, by today's standards it would be an unbackable management team. Nobody would invest in them. Larry Ellison couldn't raise venture money because nobody would invest in this team. But if you look at the dynamic that's there, I think Larry Ellison was this very creative, very driven, very, very aggressive, and very charismatic professional. Bob Minor, who was one of the finest people I have ever met in my life, with just good, sound core values, was an incredibly talented engineer. Bob served as the conscience of the company. Without Bob in that role, there would have been a great imbalance.

As the numbers got bigger and bigger and things became harder and harder and the systems in Oracle became more and more strained, I think that there was pressure from the top to engage in activities that were more and more questionable. From the top down, any means would justify the end. This became a moral dilemma for me. I didn't want to be part of it. It was just something I personally couldn't stomach anymore, so I left the company. I took a leave of absence because that was the easiest way out.

At the time I left I don't think I created an enemy in Larry. I think that happened a little bit later when Siebel achieved some degree of success in the application software business.

I was actually writing the business plan for what would have later become Siebel Systems when I left Oracle. But I was contacted by a headhunter and recruited to be the chief executive officer of a company called Cayenne Systems; it was kind of an obscure name. And so I went there instead.

"Cayenne" was an unusual name, and the founders had some pride in it, but I did not think it was the most effective name for what the company wanted to accomplish and so we renamed the company Gain Technology, and that was a great professional experience.

We were a leader in the multimedia field. We allowed organizations to build large-scale multiuser applications that incorporated a wide range of media types—sound, motion, graphics, video, text, hypertext, or what have you; we were very much a leader in multimedia. And that was a great experience. We had great customers. It was a great place to work. We had incredibly talented employees.

I was chief executive. One thing led to another; we got in some strategic alliance discussions with a company called Sybase, which at the time was a very successful database company. Ultimately, we decided to put the two companies together. We basically sold Gain to Sybase. I think it was about a two-year effort.

Founding Siebel

If we look at the business of information technology and what we had done successfully up to about the mid-'90s, we had successfully applied the information technology to change the way we work, the way that we play, the way that we entertain ourselves. We had changed the way we manufacture products. We had changed the way that we handle accounting systems, the way that

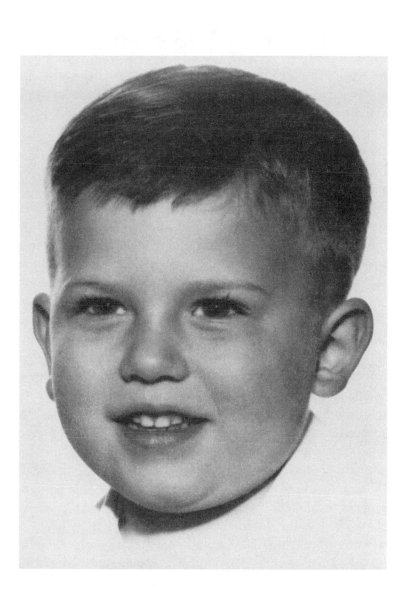

*Sign here: Even as a boy, supersalesman
Tom Siebel's focus was unmistakable.*

we handle productivity solutions in companies, the way that we manage our personnel through human resources systems. And yet if we look at the problem of sales/marketing/customer service, as recently as the beginning and middle of this decade, it was a problem that was largely untouched by the application of information technology. The state of the art in customer service, the state of the art in sales automation was still people, you know, writing on yellow stickies and Post-it notes or the note scribbled on the back of a business card.

It was absolutely clear to me, as a subscriber to this theory of this postindustrial society, that people would apply information technology to the customer management process. So we set out to basically build a software architecture and a complete solution based upon modern technology that would allow organizations to apply information and communication technology to the problem of establishing and maintaining customer relationships.

Pat House cofounded the business with me: She's the executive vice president at Siebel Systems. Pat and I founded the business together. Pat and I had worked together at Oracle Corporation for some years, and then we had been associates in the business when I was an executive at Gain. Pat is a person for whom I had developed enormous professional respect. Pat is without a question one of the most talented people in the information technology business, certainly the most talented person with whom I've had an opportunity to work in my professional career. This company would not be where it is today without Pat House. But the fact that she was a female was absolutely irrelevant in any of the discussions, in any of the thought processes, and, honestly, it's irrelevant today.

I called her on a car phone from a restaurant in MacArthur Park in Palo Alto. I told her in three minutes what the premise of this company was going to be and I said it's time we start this company. She said, count me in, when do you want to get together, and I said, well, why don't we do it right now. She came over to the house and we went into the library. We sketched out the product architecture, the business plan, and the long-term strategy, which, by and large, is pretty much what we're still executing today. That's how Siebel got started.

Pat had been very successful in her professional career at Oracle and Frame. So the fact of the matter is, we didn't need money. And I think the venture capital community serves an enormous service in the business, in financing companies, in providing leadership to companies and providing connections to these companies. But we didn't need the leadership, we didn't need the connections, we didn't need the money.

So in our case, if we called somebody for a meeting I think that we were probably going to get the meeting because we had known people in the business for some years. This was a business that was easily financed without venture capital.

Now the way that we did it, we didn't spend very much money. We had the crummiest space in Silicon Valley; our offices were in East Palo Alto. It was, I think, 11 cents a square foot for the office space. All of our furniture was the crummiest furniture that we could buy at auction. We wanted to approach the problem with very high levels of professionalism.

The objective here was to build a great company, was to build one of the world's leading companies. And the people that we attracted to the business and the people that we maintained in the business were really highly trained professionals, professionals in every respect. And so in the way that we comported ourselves, the way that we dressed, the way that we dealt with the customers, the way we dealt with technology issues, marketing issues, we thought professionalism was a very important aspect.

The dot-com start-up cultures are appropriate cultures for what those companies are accomplishing. But what we set out to do, building a large, global, leading enterprise in its space, would require a group of pretty tried, tested, proven, and experienced professionals to execute that business plan.

We were always building a large, global company. Even though there were 5 of us, there were 10 of us, there were 20 of us, we were never building a Silicon Valley start-up nor were we building a company with the idea that we might do an IPO someday. Our objective was to build a large, global, leading company in the area of customer management systems, sales/marketing/customer service. So we brought in people capable of managing large, global enterprises, and we've put in the infrastructure and the systems to manage a large, global enterprise.

We've never been focused upon market valuation. When you come in our lobby, there's no ticker tape that shows what the stock price is today. Our sole, driving, core focus is to build one of the world's great companies; this is why we're here.

For the first 18 months [the employees] worked for no salary. They worked for just pure equity. It turned out to be a pretty good investment. Several hundred employees became millionaires. A fundamental premise of this company is that we wanted it to be an employee-owned company. This was like a Marxist dream. We wanted the workers to own the means of production. And in a funny way we have this incredible, capitalist success story that was . . . the workers own the means of production. And this is what we wanted.

This was never about making money. It was never about going public; it was never about the creation of wealth. This was about an attempt to build an incredibly high-quality company. I suppose if I was a great musician that maybe I would play the guitar, if I was a great golfer maybe I would go out on tour, but I can't play the piano and my golf game is pretty horrible. So what I think, frequently under those circumstances, what you do is do what you do best. And I think that maybe what I do best is start and operate information technology companies.

As part of our start-up strategy for Siebel Systems, a core component was to establish a clear thought leadership position in this space. We wanted to establish thought leadership, very similar to what Chuck Schwab has done in brokerage or perhaps Bill Gates has done in his field. We worked together to publish the books in the space; first, the book *Virtual Selling* and then later *Cyber Rules*. We give the keynote addresses at industry conferences, we publish magazines; we wanted to establish a clear thought leadership in this space.

When we got into this business in 1993, this area for sales/marketing/customer service was highly fragmented and nobody was succeeding. There was not a very clear road map to the industry and to these companies about where to go or how to succeed.

We wanted companies to succeed in this space. We wanted to succeed ourselves, and what we have tried to do for the industry, for the customers, and, indeed, for our competitors, is to provide a clear road map as to where we thought this technology was going. That means we have to move pretty fast, because we're telling everybody where we're going and how to get there. A number of companies have been following this leadership position and have now been quite successful in the space.

It's a very competitive market and I think that today we might be able to stumble, but two years ago if we had stumbled it would have been a big problem.

We're in a dramatically different business today than we were in 1995. And we have changed very quickly to meet the needs of the market. The confluence of internetwork computing and software agent technology is going to be a very, very interesting phenomenon. When we get into virtual buying agents and virtual selling agents interacting over the 'Net, independent of the people or the organizations that they represent, this is going to get very exciting.

Core Values

I think that if we look at recent years, Oracle devoted all their rhetoric and all their energy to destroying Bill Gates at Microsoft, and now they're devoting all their rhetoric and all their energy and all their marketing dollars to destroying Lou Gerstner at IBM. As I look around, it doesn't look like all these sticks and stones have had too much of an effect on toppling Bill Gates or Lou Gerstner. It looks to me like this is a bunch of noise in the market, and we pretty much ignore it and go about our business.

Oracle has been very vocal in this space now since about 1995. If and when Oracle delivers . . . I mean, Oracle's a great company, they're well managed, they have talented people, and if and when they deliver a functionally complete competitive product in this space they'll become a competitor in the market. To date they've not succeeded at doing that. I think they've done a pretty good job with all this rhetoric. I congratulate them as a marketing organization because with all this rhetoric they've given themselves the appearance of credibility in the market. And so I think it's working for them as a marketing ploy.

What makes me a good salesman is that by training I'm an engineer. There were times at Oracle when I served in sales capacities, and during those times I did pretty well. The process of selling information technology is not about glad-handing, it's not about cajoling, it's not about really even persuading. The process of selling information technology is, most importantly engaging in a dialogue to understand what an individual's or an organization's information requirements are. Then you explain quite thoroughly, quite concisely, and quite accurately how the technologies that you might have available can be applied to some of those problems completely. People who can do that well tend to excel at information technology sales. To the extent that I succeeded in selling information technology, I think it was through that skill set.

When you peel away all the layers of the onion and look at why a company's core people are succeeding year after year after year, it's not because of their golf game and it's not because of the three-martini lunches and the backslapping and kind of the sycophant type of behavior. The reason why people excel is that they have a thorough understanding of their products, their market, and their customers' information technology or product requirements, whatever the industry may be. They can explain in context how their products can be applied to solve that customer's problem. Our strategy at Siebel is to apply information technology and communications technology to dramatically improve people's ability to communicate in this fashion.

Fame is one of the trappings of the success of the business. But money and fame have changed my life very little. I live in the same house I lived in when I was at Oracle in the early days. We live in the same town. Our kids go to the same school. The kids are getting a little older. I don't work any less. I think the biggest aspect that has changed my life is that I travel a lot more. And that is difficult to balance with the needs of family, which are important. Especially with babies and little boys and girls, that's a challenge.

I probably travel 60 percent of the time, and I'm out visiting customers, and the customers are all over the world. And we're absolutely committed that we're going to do whatever it takes to make sure every one of these customers succeeds. That is a cornerstone of our corporate culture, and I personally involved myself in that process a lot. But weekends are for the family. Every weekend we're together as a family. We may go someplace, we may stay home, but pretty much every weekend is with them, and this is how we reconcile it.

Public recognition is not something that we're seeking out, but it is happening. I think that [being] offered up as a role model to other individuals who want to follow a path that you carved is humbling.

Some responsibility is put on your shoulders to try to set an example to communicate core values that might benefit other people. My core values are building a quality company, doing whatever it takes to make sure the customer succeeds, treating employees well, and trying to build a working environment that is perceived as great.

You see many chief executives focused on being great visionaries or makers of insanely great technology or these great entrepreneurs or all that silliness. I recognize what's really taking place here. What's taking place here is, we are living in Silicon Valley in the midst of an economic miracle unprecedented in the history of mankind. Many of us find ourselves here in the right place at the right time and have been enormously fortunate.

This is the professional experience of a lifetime. It has been, and continues to be, enormously rewarding and fulfilling. What I want to do with my career is do everything I can to try to lead Siebel Systems to be a recognized leader, a company of the same caliber as a Daimler-Benz and General Electric, IBM—a great, great company.

For someone starting out today, my advice would be to work for a larger company for a few years and learn how it's done. See how it's managed and learn some skills. I would go work for a Hewlett-Packard, I would go work for an IBM, I would go work for a Sun Microsystems. I would go to work for a Siebel Systems; I'd go to work for a high-quality, well-managed company and I would learn how it's done. Learn some skills, sales organizations, and marketing organizations, and not only learn what's done right, but what's done wrong. Maybe the most important thing you learn at one of these companies is what they do wrong. And then take that out and go. I don't think, right out of college, I would do one of these start-ups.

Real entrepreneurs know when to leave and start their own company. They have a biological clock, an entrepreneurial clock in there ticking, and they just go do it. When the time comes, you just have to go do it. You might succeed or you might fail, but I think that when that moment comes, they move.

☰

Since this interview, Siebel Systems has continued to enjoy a historical ramp-up in sales and profits, though its stock, which flew with the dot-coms, took a nasty shot along with all the other enterprise software giants. Still, the company has continued to grow, with current revenues exceeding $1.14 billion (for the six months ending 6/30/01).

Despite his success, Tom Siebel is still running the company on a day-to-day basis. On the rare occasions when I hear from him, it is from a plane racing to the East Coast or Europe or the Far East.

Why is he still working so hard? The answer may be down the highway a couple of miles: Larry Ellison and Oracle. Ellison has publicly declared war on his old VP, and the two firms are now locked in one of the most epic battles in high-tech history. Hundreds of billions of dollars rest on the results of this fight. And it will be to the death, because neither man is accustomed to giving quarter.

Bill Gates
Cofounder, Chief Software Architect, and Chairman, Microsoft

The Man
- Born on October 28, 1955
- Raised in Seattle, Washington
- Studied at Harvard University, left as a junior
- Married, two children

The Entrepreneur
- Cofounded Microsoft in 1975
- Built the company into a software empire and his wealth to a level that surpassed everyone else on the planet
- Microsoft year 2000 revenues: $21 billion (fiscal year ending 12/31/00)

"There's still a lot of those horizons. The reason you come in every day is that the days themselves are fun, not because there's some grand triumph at the end of it."

$\mathcal{W}$henever the heavyweight champion of the world enters any room, he knows that he can whip anyone in the place—and everyone in the room knows it, too. The same can be said of one of the world's richest people. No matter how long you've known him, or how graciously he treats you, that one fact forever colors your dealings with him.

William H. (Bill) Gates was the last interview of the television series, and, as you might expect, the hardest to schedule. Like Larry Ellison and Scott McNealy, Gates demanded that we come to him—that is, to Redmond, Washington—and do the shoot in Microsoft's studios.

There were good and bad features to the location. The good was that MS's television facility was better than most television production studios (including network) I'd ever seen. The bad was that, with the exception of Bob Grove in the control room, the shooters would all be Microsoft employees. In other words, their paychecks were signed by our guest.

Luckily, despite his public image as a master puppeteer pulling the strings of millions of minions, Gates's presence among his employees evoked none of the fear we saw with Ellison at Oracle. There was a little of the "Elvis has entered the auditorium" environment. The cameramen became a little more crisp and circumspect upon Gates's arrival, but otherwise it was business as usual.

Going in, I knew I faced a big challenge. How do you get Bill Gates to relax and open up? Connie Chung tried by asking Gates about his business practices . . . and watched him walk off the set. Others have tried different tacks and ended up in the middle of a charmless, impersonal reading of complex technology and business clichés.

I wasn't particularly intimidated by Gates: We've known each other for 20 years. Our first encounter was sitting at the same table at Arnaud's in New Orleans during a technology conference in 1980. I was a young reporter then, and he was an even younger entrepreneur making his first big public appearance. In the years since, I've attacked him in *Upside* magazine and defended him in the *Wall Street Journal*, and he has written a couple articles for me in *Forbes* ASAP.

Bob Grove was even less awestruck. A decade ago, filming a television show with Gates, Grove had casually reached over, plucked Gates's grimy glasses from his nose, and cleaned them on his own shirttail.

But how to get one of the most guarded men in the world to drop his guard?

The interview began slowly and predictably. I asked business questions, and Gates replied with the usual stock answers. I felt like a dumb trade-press reporter. Fifteen minutes in, knowing I was running out of time, I decided to go deep. Sitting on the set, as a kind of standard Microsoft prop, was an original Altair 8800, the first personal computer, the product of Gates's first employer, and the machine he and Paul Allen had first designed "MicroSoft" BASIC for. As it happened, almost 25 years before, I had been at the trade show in San Francisco that featured the Altair (and introduced the Apple II). Gates was there, too, but we did not meet.

Taking a flyer, I began to ask him about the Altair. It was as if a wall had suddenly crumbled. Gates's eyes lit up. Now we were talking about something he cared deeply about. That I was also a survivor of that era only made the conversation warmer. Suddenly we were in the digital version of a VFW hall, sitting on adjoining bar stools, telling old war stories. The only difference was, I had covered the battles as a mere correspondent. Gates, on the other hand, had won the war. Still, it was enough. The rest of the conversation, which ranged from his childhood to his early days in technology, showed a different Bill Gates than I, or most anybody else, had ever seen. Afterwards, members of the studio crew came up to tell me that they'd never seen Gates so comfortable.

How did we break through such a prickly exterior? I wish I could say it was my interviewing style or our common history. But I suspect that just as important was timing: Gates, still being battered by the Justice Department on antitrust issues, had just stepped down as Microsoft CEO, retaining only his title of chairman, and announced he was going back to the lab. Thus, we had caught him at a major turning point in his life. Married, with two children, after a year of seeing his name besmirched in every newspaper on earth, I suspect Bill Gates was taking stock of his career and life when we sat down. The interview merely tapped into a powerful current that was just beneath the surface.

≋

I'm curious. We're a week away from this rather stunning announcement you made that you're stepping down from the driver's seat at Microsoft. I was trying to think of a precedent for that, and I couldn't think of anyone who's done what you just did.

Well, I've been running Microsoft for over 25 years, from the early days of the vision and writing most of the software myself, to hiring people in and creating a company that was designed around the idea of software. That was really what made us so different. We were the first to have the idea of how the industry could be structured around the PC.

But the thing that we knew, the thing that we loved, was software, and how you could build a company that would bring great people in to do that. So for 25 years, I've done that. The company's gotten to be a good-sized company, but nowhere near the size of an IBM. In terms of employees, we're about an eighth of IBM. But even so, it's over 30,000 people now.

We have a lot of challenges—the consulting efforts we provide for our customers, the scalability, reliability, speech recognition, handwriting recognition, getting what we call the natural interface. And I've chosen now to focus in on those product decisions, and let Steve [Ballmer]—who's been here with me about 20 years—be the CEO. He's a great businessman. I'm very lucky to have him.

I'm certainly still very much in the thick of things in terms of what I really like, which is: What products are we going to do? How are we going to get the tablet machine [a new Microsoft handheld terminal] out there? How do we get people to redesign their web sites so that voice interaction can work the right way? How do we get security so that people feel like they can give up paper contracts and paper bills and just trust that the network does it the right way and preserves their privacy? There's deep technical issues behind all of those things.

I enjoyed being CEO. I enjoyed making the business and organizational decisions. But you really have to specialize. If I want to design this next generation and really motivate all the kid engineers, I need to spend full time on it. And so, in my 40s, I decided that I'd change my role.

I'll be very involved in all the choices and trade-offs we make. I probably won't write much code. You know, I sometimes threaten to when I say, "Geez, this ought to be easy. I could come in this weekend and do something like this." But I'll still be very, very hands on.

Growing Up

Seattle was fairly dependent in the '60s on Boeing. And as the aerospace industry went through a downturn there, it was fairly tough. Now, you know, Seattle is a strong beneficiary of this economy. We've got lots of great biotech firms here. We've got Amazon here. We've got all sorts of companies that have been part of this new wave.

Seattle is a great city, and one of the reasons we've been able to hire such a great workforce is that the quality of life up here is very, very high.

My father is a large man, and a serious attorney. He actually ran his own law firm. Both my folks were involved in an incredible range of things. My mom pretty early on got involved in a lot of community things and ended up being on the board of the University of Washington and the phone company and an insurance company and a lot of very interesting things. She was incredibly energetic, lots of activities in the household. She clearly wanted her kids to take school seriously, and she signed us up for more activities than we could think of.

They were good at sharing what they were up to at dinner at night, talking about United Way and the challenges it faced, or various lawsuits. My dad always was talking about the challenges he had, as though, you know, it was interesting for me to hear about it. I might even have had something to say about it. They included us. They took us on trips. We'd read the same books that our parents were reading.

And they had a lot of interesting friends, some of whom went on to have great success in politics and some other things. So I lived in a very stimulating environment. I was encouraged to read. My parents were nice enough to send me to a pretty good school, partly because I'd been getting really bad grades, and they thought it was at odds with my potential. I was very, very good at tests, but at school, I wasn't that engaged.

That's partly why they sent me to what, at the time, was a private boys' school with a heavy emphasis on kids staying focused. It probably was good for me. It's there that the very first computer terminal showed up. I got very engaged in that thing [computers], so I give my parents a lot of credit. They encouraged me, giving me a sense of confidence. And then exposing me to what was going on out at Lakeside School, I think, made a big difference.

I have two sisters. My older sister is just a couple of years older than I am, so we basically grew up together. My younger sister is nine years younger, and so when I was in high school, she was still pretty young.

My older sister got great grades right up to the day she discovered boys, and then I became the scholar of the house. It was an interesting transition because Christy had always gotten straight A's. There was this thing where if somebody got straight A's, everybody got to go out to dinner at some nice place. There was literally never a year that didn't happen, because just when she got a little bit distracted, then I had finally decided that, "Okay, I'm going to get good grades this year." So I actually read the stuff and turned my stuff in and did pretty well at it. I always liked school, but it took some teachers at Lakeside to kind of get me engaged in really caring about what they were talking about.

In my younger years, I tried to be the class clown. Because that's where you got the most attention. But at Lakeside, they actually liked people who sort of were serious about their studies.

I remember one time they were giving this quiz, and they were pairing people up. They paired me with this guy that I thought knew nothing. And I thought, "Oh, no! Are they confused? Do they think I don't know, I don't understand this stuff?" And that was part of deciding, "Okay, I'll get serious about my studies." Then there was the whole matter of what college I'd go to. Eventually I figured out, "Oh, if you don't get very good grades, you're going to be stuck not going to as good a school," and that has follow-up effects potentially for the rest of your life.

I was sent once to a professional to get some help. I'm sure there were a lot of different things, but what I really got out of it was a sense of all my energies. What did I want to focus on? Did I want to focus on proving that I didn't really care about the rules and what my parents were trying to impose on me? Or should I focus my energies on kind of learning neat new things? Or some of the sports stuff? And so it was kind of a turning point in saying that the outside world was where the challenge was. It was about the time that I got sent to Lakeside, and an environment where I had to pay attention.

I remember taking the entrance exam and deciding, "Hey, I don't really want to go to this place because they're really going to discipline me. And, you know, it would be easy to fail the entrance exam." But my sister and I had always talked about tests, and how we can do well on tests. So I just had too much pride. I decided I was going to do well on this test, particularly all these math questions that my sister and I had always talked about that we felt we were ahead on. Then I got accepted and I thought, "Geez, did I make a real mistake, passing this entrance exam?" But you know, in retrospect, having a school with small classes and really good teachers was a great thing for me. And then there was the serendipity that they actually had a computer terminal out there that the teachers were intimidated by. So it was myself and a few of my friends who became the experts in what the heck this computer terminal could do.

That is also where I met Paul Allen. In school you mostly hang around with people in your own class. But when this terminal arrived, there were people of all ages who were kind of trying to figure out what to do with it. And I'd say there were five or six of us who were incredibly intense. It cut across age boundaries. Paul was two years older than me, and we met at the computer terminal. Paul wanted to figure it out. I had done very well at math, and so I also had this notion that, "Hey, I can figure these things out." Paul kept challenging me. He kept saying, "Can you figure this part out? Can you figure this part out?" Unlike some people, he really wanted to understand the thing. And so he and I became very close friends, and, in the long run, we were the ones who were the most addicted or involved in the whole computer thing, staying late at

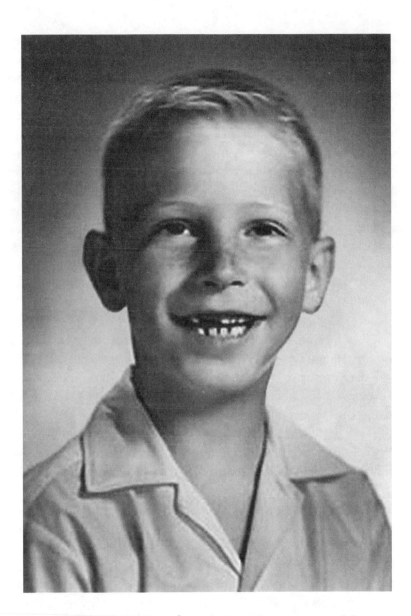

All grins: Ladies and gentlemen, the most powerful and feared businessman on the planet.

night. Eventually we got jobs from computer companies to work part-time, even though we were in our early teens.

We formed a group. Paul had a friend, and I had a friend. So there were four of us. We called ourselves Lakeside Programming Group. We were in the ninth grade. And we took on some projects. And then, when I was in tenth grade, my very, very close friend, Kent Evans, was killed in a mountain-climbing accident. There were a lot of things we had been working on.

Paul and I eventually had to just work that much harder to fulfill the commitments. And then Paul and I took over doing the class scheduling for the high school. They'd actually had a teacher try and do it, but it was a very complex problem, and that had basically failed. So there was a year where the school was chaos, because nobody knew which class they were supposed to be in. So Paul and I worked on that in the summer.

The story is that you programmed the schedule to get into class with the most girls.

That's no myth. We had by then merged with a girls' school, but there was still about a 3-to-1 ratio, boys to girls. And so when I did the history sections, just by coincidence, I set it with 12 girls and just a couple other guys—but pretty wimpy guys—in one history section. So doing the schedule had its benefits. We also got paid to do it, and it was a deep problem. It was an interesting dream come true. I recommend it.

Ninth grade was the year when I decided to get straight A's and be serious. And so I had this whole thing where I sat in the back of the class, in the back corner, never answered a question unless I was called on, and just sort of, you know, virtually memorized the book. I just read it three or four times. And then there were these early tests, PSAT or something, and I got perfect scores on that stuff. So by then I was certainly out in the open in terms of my intellectual ambition and desire to read and everything like that. That's when this whole computer thing came along, and I ended up teaching the computer classes, because the teachers had been intimidated by the thing. They even had me take over teaching some of their math sections.

And so, by now, I was thought of as a real student. And then there was an interesting turn where I was offered a job working on this incredible project to computerize the power grid of the Northwest, with the Bonneville Power Administration.

It was a very challenging project. So I would have been—let's see—I would have been about 15 when I was offered the job, and 16 when I took it. So there was the question: Would my parents let me take part of my senior year off and go work a few hours away down in Vancouver, Washington? And, you know, my parents wondered: Would it affect my school admission?

It was a funny deal. What happened was [that] this project was in deep trouble. TRW had contracted to get the thing done on a certain schedule, and it just wasn't getting done, and it was very complicated. And so Bonneville kept asking, "Who understands these computers? These Digital Equipment's PDP 10s?" And TRW said, "Well . . ."

At school Paul and I had been finding problems in the PDP 10 operating system, and we'd just been sending in the problem reports. At first we were just sort of banging on the system, finding random problems. But eventually we got the source code out of a garbage can and studied it. So our problem reports eventually were very sophisticated, you know, like: This is how you fix this problem. And as long as you're in this module, you might as well improve this here. So people back at Digital Equipment's headquarters in Boston knew there were two kids in Washington that were very smart about this operating system. Finally when TRW was saying to Digital, "Oh, we've got to get more experts in. We've got to get experts in," somebody said, "Well, there's always Gates and Allen. Those guys know this operating system cold." And everybody said, "Who are they? Where are they? Nobody ever met these guys. Who are these guys?" And one guy said, "I know who they are. I'll get 'em." So, anyway, he had us come in for an interview, and everybody goes, "Wait a minute. These are kids."

But they really wanted to hire us. So they offered us a huge salary and everything. It was a dream job, because I would diagnose all these problems. I would stay up all night. And I had the whole computer all to myself. It was just a dream job. And it was an incredible project. I mean, the reliability requirements for these power projects are almost beyond the state of the art—very hard stuff.

Cambridge Bound

While I was working there, in January, I heard back early from some of the colleges I had applied to—Harvard, Princeton, Yale . . .

Actually, in retrospect, in terms of good weather, it would have been nice to go to Stanford. Those Boston winters were a little cold for me. I wasn't ready for it. And the size, you know—Harvard was pretty big. I came from a school where I had 100 people in my entire graduating class. I had been, the last three or four years, kind of the math/science/computer guy. I knew who I was. Then I went to Harvard, and everybody in my first math class got 800 on the SAT. Everybody. We're all the Math Guy. We also know that, out of 80 people in the class, like 40 of us are probably substandard [*laughs*]. That was kind of intimidating. But, you know, I wanted to go to the East Coast. I thought it would be good exposure. I wanted to go to a school that wasn't just science. So, although I'd gone and visited MIT, I didn't end up applying there. I had this thing about going to the East Coast, you know, meet the kids from other schools who had done well on all these math tests over the years, and kind of try out different things.

I'd be surprised if freshmen going into Harvard don't have some part of the time when they felt like, "Wow! This is incredible. Where do I fit in? What is it that I'm doing here?" Those first few years there, which were about all I got, I was trying to figure out what I wanted to focus on. I took a lot of economics classes. I took a lot of psychology classes. I wasn't quite sure. Was I going to end up with my computer thing? Going into Harvard, I hadn't thought so, because computers weren't mainstream. But then again, we saw that they could become mainstream.

It wasn't like I was forced to make a decision. The nice thing about Harvard is there's all those smart kids just hanging out and doing nothing. And so there's no shortage of people to just hang out and talk about the world and your parents and how things are.

I was the opposite of a party animal. I mean, I had this thing where if I was signed up for a class, I wouldn't go to the class, *ever*. My position was, "Okay, I get good grades, but I don't try at all. I never go to the actual classes." And I would just sit around and talk about stuff. I learned a little about procrastination that I had to unlearn later as I got into the real world.

Harvard is where I met Steve Ballmer. Steve was different than I was. Steve was involved in campus activities. He was in the clubs. He and I were a little bit opposites, because I was sort of against all the campus stuff. I thought, "Those people are just trying to put it on their resume. Let's just hang out." Steve had so much energy. He's just his raw talent and his incisiveness. In our dorm — Steve and I ended up in the same dorm — there were people who hung around Steve, and there were people who hung around me. Well, there was this one guy who liked us both and kept saying, "You got to meet each other." And the first time we met, you know, it was kind of like, "Well, you're in all this campus stuff. What kind of guy are you?" He was sort of the ultimate middle-class guy who comes from Detroit and decides that he's going to make good at Harvard. And I kept giving him a hard time about that. I was sort of the prototype of, you know, the kid who sort of comes and says, "I'm not going to get swept up in all of this stuff." I was taking a lot of nice classes, but still not sure where I was going with all of it.

Now, Paul — Paul, of course, because he's two years older than me — he'd gone to Washington State University, when I was working in my senior year. He was taking time off from that. Then when I went back to Cambridge, he and I wanted to brainstorm together. He also needed to get a job. So I did this thing where I interviewed at a company, and said, "Well, if you want to hire me, you have to hire my friend." *[Laughs.]* And he's 3,000 miles away. So they would have to interview him by phone.

But they hired him. So Paul had a job. Now he could move out to Boston and be with me and kind of brainstorm during those years I was at Harvard. We kept talking about, "Hey, you know, is the revolution going to happen that we've talked about? Should we do a company? Or should we just go and do more mainstream things? Be an economist, a lawyer, a mathematician, a scientist, that kind of thing?"

So Paul is standing in Harvard Square. There's a magazine stand there. And he always picks up *Popular Electronics.* In the back of that issue there is this Altair kit computer—what we had talked about for so long. He showed it to me. We were excited, but we also said, "God, this could happen without us." And so it was kind of scary.

Then we decided, "Look, we are going to do the software for this." We talked about this particular chip, the Intel 8080 chip that was in the Altair. Paul and I knew that we could write BASIC for it—we could do some amazing stuff with this machine. So he and I called up the company, MITS, and said, "Hey, we've got software." They said, "Some people have called up and said that." Well, then, so we worked day and night for about three months and actually wrote the BASIC, which was our first product, and Paul flew out and actually ran the BASIC on their computer. They were just blown away by that, and then they became our first customer.

So I left school. You know, colleges are great about [it] if you take a year or two off. You can always come back. Officially, I could go back at any time. So, they could tell I was very passionate about this. They were pretty supportive, in fact. And I sort of thought, "Well, I'll just go out for a year, then I can finish college, and go back." But I didn't know how intense it would get. So they didn't think of it as leaving permanently. And you know, it was in Albuquerque, New Mexico, where this MITS company was. And so Paul and I moved out there and started hiring our friends and, you know, that was the beginning of Microsoft.

At any point in our history, it would have been easy to say, you know, there's this huge challenge ahead of the company. Competing with IBM, when IBM was pushing OS2. Betting on Windows, at any point, you could look and say, "Wow, this company has some big challenges."

One thing that I have learned [from] running a company is [that] the operating instructions need the graybeards. And you need to pick the ones who have kind of the open-mindedness and the passion and that create a team approach that can take on those incredible challenges.

For a high-tech company to get through all those periods—the management turmoil, the strategy changes, going public, and stuff like that—usually you fall off a cliff at some point. Our story is almost too good to be true. You look at our sales or profits. It's just like a straight line. But underneath that, there were plenty of crises.

I always knew that my management style was to see the problems coming, and not think about, "Okay, what are we doing well?" I think about what we're *not* doing well, but in a very nonemotional way. Getting people panicked is not a way to have them rise to the challenge. Instead, it's about structuring the problem. How do we develop this skill? Do we need to partner with somebody for this? How do we make other companies successful so this thing really grows in the right way? We took those things on in a very rational way and thought ahead.

I didn't pretend I knew all the answers. I was lucky enough to hire in a lot of great people. But also, you know, learning about, "Okay, how do you grow a business? How do you get into Europe? What do you do in Japan? What about these Japanese companies? Do you work with them? How do you work with them?" You know, going around the world to figure out, "Okay, how do we adopt our software for Chinese and Korean and all these things?" Seeing the young people we hire develop into vice presidents of big groups and being very sophisticated.

And some of the competitive bouts. You really get involved in, "Can we have the most popular word processor?"—which, for a while WordPerfect was. "Can we have the most popular network operating system?" Now it's: "Can we make Windows so scalable that it finally comes and replaces mainframes?"

This is an industry that's full of companies that missed the change in the market. Take Wang. Wang was this great, wonderful company, but because they missed the transition in word processors and minicomputers, there is no Wang today. Or take Digital Equipment. More than any other company, I grew up admiring their view of time-sharing and those PDP machines that I played around with as a kid.

To have Digital Equipment bought out by Compaq, which is the company that we pioneered a lot of great PC things with, only shows that this is a business where you can miss the next trend and die.

The possibility is that this company's going to miss one eventually — hey, that's going to happen someday. There's no company in the technology business that's forever. That's partly why it's such a fun business. I mean, if this was a business like making bread, where you figure out your formula and just stick with it, I wouldn't have wanted to be CEO for 25 years. It wouldn't have kept me engaged and excited and learning new things and having to figure out how to grow the business. But because it's such a fast-changing business, I feel like every day I've been challenged to the fullest. And certainly in this new role, I'll have plenty of that challenge going forward.

I also feel some nostalgia about being able to know the source code of the product by heart, and literally every line of code, which was the case way back with BASIC. I supervised it. I made sure there was nothing wasted, nothing inconsistent, nothing wrong in any way, shape, or form. It was just totally pristine. I miss that a tiny bit, because, as products get larger, you get teams of people, and there's no way to have the perfection that the smaller products of the early days had.

Those early years with Paul were very fantastic. The kind of passion we had. The optimism. The vision of what this thing would become. I mean, you know, there's nothing more fun than that. Working with your friends to build something, seeing it come true, you know, making all sorts of mistakes, and having to fix them. There's not a thing I would change.

As often happens, the interview ended just as we were getting into it. I believe my interview actually succeeded in bringing out the real Bill Gates for the first time in public. He even graciously let the interview go on for an extra 10 minutes (while his handlers paced back and forth and muttered). Still, we found faith with the knowledge that we got as much of Gates as anybody had for a long, long time.

My wife and two sons came along for the shoot. They sat in the greenroom watching the interview, then came out just as Gates was leaving. When he saw my boys, Bill stopped, ignoring his handlers, and walked over and shook hands with them. With the smile of a new dad on his face, Gates talked to the boys for a long time, again shook their hands in turn, and rushed off.

"He's a nice man," said my oldest. I didn't know what to say.

Carol Bartz
Chairman, CEO, and President, Autodesk

The Woman
- Born on August 29, 1948
- Born in Minnesota and raised in Wisconsin
- Earned a B.S. in computer science from the University of Wisconsin, an Honorary Doctorate of Letters degree from Williams Woods University, and an Honorary Doctorate of Science degree from Worcester Polytechnic Institute
- Married, one daughter

The Entrepreneur
- Joined Autodesk in 1992
- Previously vice president of worldwide operations at Sun Microsystems
- Autodesk year 2000 revenues: $936 million (fiscal year ending 1/1/01)

"I can't think of a better thing to tell a 6-year-old, a 15-year-old, or a 45-year-old, than this: Try things you're not comfortable with."

Carol Bartz is probably the sanest entrepreneur I've ever met. Smart, brassy, caring, and tough, she is someone you'd like to go out with for a few beers and swap tales.

It is hard to know exactly where all this sanity came from. Perhaps it was her Midwestern upbringing, a surprisingly common trait among the great leaders of high tech, from David Packard to Bob Noyce to Tom Siebel, Larry Ellison, and Scott McNealy. It may also have come from the fact that she was not a class nerd but the homecoming queen, and that she didn't find her forte until she was a young adult.

One thing for certain: Her dangerous bout with cancer, which hit while she was both raising a young daughter and taking over a troubled Autodesk, did something special to her character. Perhaps, unlike the male executives on this series, some of whom have not been troubled by either the demands of fatherhood (even when they were fathers) or a sense of their own mortality, Bartz has learned to put her entrepreneurial impulses into a larger context.

I wrote at the beginning of the book that true entrepreneurs are willing to die for what they do. Certainly Carol Bartz was no different. The image of her stumbling up the steps of Autodesk on the way to her first board meeting, full of chemotherapy medicine—and stopping to vomit in the bushes—is one of the most compelling and telling in the history of high tech. Bartz wasn't standing there retching out of a sense of duty, but because she wanted to be there. She wanted Autodesk, and even the threat of death wouldn't keep her away.

And yet what makes Bartz different from her peers, I think, is that, having risked death and survived, she discovered that even though she was willing to die for her company, she didn't have to. She could be a mother and work in the garden, go out to quiet dinners and still build a strong, successful company. Perhaps that's why, on the brink of becoming the most celebrated woman CEO in America, she pulled back from the publicity and left the limelight to those, like Kim Polese, who followed her. Instead, she focused on making Autodesk, the world's leading designer of computer-aided design tools for architects and contractors, successful—and her own life complete.

My encounters with Carol Bartz usually devolve into low gossip, dirty jokes, and raucous laughter. This time we maintained a certain amount of decorum. Unfortunately for Bartz, it was a hot day, and the studio lights were even hotter. She had raced down 60 miles from Marin to get to the shoot and was rushed right onto the set. As a result, about halfway through the interview, Bartz looked like she was about to melt. The rest of the filming consisted of five minutes of talk, followed by three minutes of makeup, repeated six times. But, as always, Carol was a trouper—and once the shoot was over, we retreated to the cool darkness behind the cameras and joked for another half hour.

*It's amazing how many people, how many entrepreneurs in Sili-
con Valley, have Midwestern upbringings. You can go all the way
back to David Packard and Bob Noyce. They all grew up in the
Midwest. And you did, too, in Wisconsin. How big was this town?*

Well, it's 800 now, but it was a thousand when I lived there. I
grew up on a dairy farm. Most of us lived on the surrounding farms
and we thought we were pretty big time. The school was small and
you did a lot of activities. I was a cheerleader, drum majorette,
and student body president. During games I would lead cheers and
then when the band came out I'd just go change my clothes, do the
little half-time show, and run back and put on the red-and-white
again. I think that's why small schools are great, because everybody
has a sense of accomplishment. Being involved in all those things
in school just seemed normal. Doers do. I mean, why would you
not? I don't think that way.

I was taught that you try and grab as much as you can and you
do it. You don't complain, and when you get the job done, you find
another one to do. I always thought it was fun to be telling people
what to do! *[Laughs.]* I mean, if you're going to play in the band,
lead it. I actually have not voiced that before, but why not?

I was raised by my grandparents. My mother died when I was
eight. So I was the mom. I was clever, though. I would bring my
friends over and everybody got a room to play house in, but they had
to clean the room first. *[Laughs.]* "You get the kitchen—that's your
house, and you have the bedroom. Now, everybody cleans their
house first." *[Laughs.]* I can't really attest to the quality of the job.

I would get up in the morning, get my baby brother dressed,
and get him off to school. It didn't seem like a lot of responsibility
at that time. You do what you do.

I went at 12 to live with my grandparents. My brother was six
years younger, so we both went. They thought it was time to let me
focus on school and less on housework and that sort of stuff.

In school, I loved math. Loved math. Nobody told me you
weren't supposed to get A's in everything, so why would math be
any different? There were only a couple of us girls that went into

the advanced geometry and trig and so forth. I just never thought it was an option to not do math. And then, when you like something, you like to do more of it.

Little girls aren't usually interested in math. I really do think they get dissuaded. I think they have too many people telling them it's not important—then they maybe hit some tough times. I also think they need to learn differently.

I worry a lot about that. Besides my gardening, I have two passions—one is cancer and truly trying to help people, everything from research through helping cancer victims. But my second passion is my biggest passion, actually: little girls and math. I will put a lot of resources in my life to trying to figure out what exactly is the problem.

I have an 11-year-old, and I'm watching this sort of firsthand. I'll tell you, she went from third grade not really knowing her times tables, to being in sixth grade in honors math. And this change happened because my husband and I really decided to focus on it and get excited with her.

I just think it was about how we approached it with her. And now, she thinks math is her easiest subject. She was on a trajectory to believe that she was not good in math.

My grandmother is still living. We're going to celebrate her 95th birthday in October, and she's a pistol. She always asks me, "What's wrong with the stock price? What are you doing today?"

I get a lot of advice from her, believe me. It's not quite that direct, but she goes, "Now, are you—are you working hard right now? 'Cause it looks like you've got a big job to do." That's the thing with Midwesterners, you know, you don't ever let down.

She's just crazy! Two years ago she bought a treadmill, because it was too snowy that year to get outside. I said, "How do you know what a treadmill is? You're, you know, 93 years old." She said "Well, why wouldn't I know what a treadmill is?" So I stopped asking.

I think she's really proud of me. She has a lot of fun showing her cronies pictures and any TV things I do. She can't believe my company's bigger than her town. Until she actually saw me at the president-elect's summit, on TV with the Washington crowd, it really hadn't sunk in.

My favorite story of her is when I was in my early teens, there was a rattlesnake up in the rafters in the barn. I went into the house and said, "Grandma, there's a rattlesnake." So she came out and looked at it, took a shovel, flipped it off the rafter, cut its head off, and said, "You could've done that."

After graduating from this small high school, I actually went to a small school in Missouri that had about 1,000 students. Frankly, for those two years, I was in that sort of "do everything" situation again. I realized that I needed more in the last couple of years of school and transferred to the University of Wisconsin, which was about 40,000 kids.

I took my first computer course and absolutely fell in love. I went wild. I had so much fun. It was an IBM 1620 card-to-tape system. We had to toggle it to boot it up. I remember my first program was to add up all the license plate numbers in Missouri. And I just thought this was fabulous, to be able to do this. This was in the late 1960s. The class was mostly men, but it was so new for everybody; what was more interesting at that time, to me, was [that] most of my classmates were in master's programs.

They were graduate students taking the same courses I did. My friend took two or three courses different than I did and got a master's in computer science, and I got a bachelor's; back then, I think there were only a couple of universities offering undergraduate computer science degrees.

We were running in fast company, but it was new to everybody. I think that because of the newness, somewhat like Silicon Valley, it was exciting; it wasn't like an old engineering program. It wasn't like you were going into a department that had been in existence forever and, "What is a female doing here?" It was a new department, it was exciting for everybody; even the professors were young.

A big problem at the time was that we were considered establishment and I had very liberal roommates. That actually was tougher than the male/female thing. I was always asked, "What are

*Duet: A successful young businesswoman
and the grandmother who raised her.*

you doing in that kind of job? You should be in psychology, sociology, government, or some sort of thing."

They had to shut down the lab during the Kent State spring, the napalm stuff, and the Dow Chemical riots. The good news was that there were a couple of courses where they couldn't give us finals . . .

After Wisconsin I went to work with 3M. That was my first exposure to "You're a woman, what are you doing here?" because I was the first woman in our division. That was very tricky. As a matter of fact, the first week there, I was actually fired. We were on a business trip and I was the only woman. They got mixed up and they roomed me with somebody. They got that sorted out, and then somebody did some rumoring, and they said, "Well, we have to fire you."

They rehired me the next morning, but that showed how strange the whole phenomenon was at the time. They wanted me for my computer science and for my background; they just didn't know what to do with a woman. Ultimately, I left 3M because they wouldn't promote me because I was a woman.

Still, I think it's a good company. I'm not trying to trash 3M here, because that was 30 years ago. But it was tough times for me.

I knew I really wanted to get into a computer company, even though I was doing systems work at 3M. I took a job at Digital Equipment Corporation (DEC). At the time, to be a salesperson there you had to be an engineer or a computer science graduate. So that was me. And there were two women in the sales force when I joined.

That was the heyday of the PDP series, before VAXs. It was really a lot of fun. I knew that if you did great things and could exhibit yourself somehow, you could just get bigger and bigger jobs. That was really cool. The company had such growth, if you were a combination of outspoken, smart, and willing to take some risks, you could go anywhere.

In those days everything was about the technology. DEC didn't pay commissions, so our whole idea at the time was to really learn how to take care of the customer and really do pretty straightforward marketing, not the level of hype that you see in today's marketing. Everything was more grounded; it was fundamentals. To me, it was Computer Marketing/Selling/Engineering 101.

I was at DEC seven years. By the time I left, I was product line manager for their OEM business. A great position.

I left DEC because California is where it was at. You could just drive down the street in California and see all those companies. Everything was in our field.

Some friends of mine moved out to Sun Microsystems. They basically encouraged me to come out and see it. It was just hot. I said, "You know, I could spend 20 more years here on the East Coast and retire, or I could go where the action is." And I thought, "How can you make a mistake? If you don't make it at Sun, you walk across the street and you try somebody else," which, of course, with the Valley, you could.

My husband and I both worked for DEC and we both went to work for Sun, which was a small start-up at the time. Sun was our life. Absolute life. And it was a fabulous time in the Valley.

I went on to run the federal division and had just a great time. We weren't known in Washington, so I really got to shake Washington up with this start-up, new technology. I was pregnant at the time—that was a good one. Here I am to sell my wares to all the agencies. That was fun.

Being a woman in the Valley was still being a minority. I only worked with men, so I was pretty good at that. And again, it was about excitement, and the market, and what competition you were taking out, and how you were going to position something new. People didn't spend a whole lot of time trying to figure out that I wore a skirt. I didn't spend a lot of time figuring out I was wearing a skirt.

I was a VP at Sun. My job was here in the Valley, and my home was in Dallas because my husband lived in Dallas. Scott McNealy said I could do my job from anywhere, but I did it in Silicon Valley.

I don't think that's unusual. A lot of these things, people hold them up and say, "Isn't this strange?" Then they make me admit it's strange: At the time, it just seemed like, why wouldn't I do that? Because I felt I could have the best of both worlds. When I went back to Dallas, I was not a high-tech exec. I was a mom. I could go to Gymboree, and I had a great time. And I had my garden.

Actually, it was a great life. I worked for a fabulous company, had a great daughter, and a great husband. They happened to be in different places; I just dealt with it. I had a great, fabulous nanny; she actually stayed with me for 10 years. Having a child was wonderful because it gave me this other thing to do besides work.

I wasn't looking to leave Sun. And, yes, headhunters pitched me—that is how these things work. I was really interested in software. I had spent my life in the hardware side, or the system side of the business, and software was very interesting to me.

Autodesk needed management and at the time I thought it was a great franchise—underutilized, undermanaged. The customers loved the software. It's not an occasional-use product. They use it to create the things in this world, so it's really meaningful. Most of the office buildings in the United States right now are designed on Autodesk software. If they're not done by hand, they're probably done on our software. The tallest buildings in the world, all the infrastructure, most of the mechanical assemblies you're seeing— it's real stuff. And I like that. I like that a lot.

I like technical markets because people make long, meaningful decisions to be your customer. They don't flip in and out every six months.

So here I was, the CEO of a company that was experiencing financial troubles, with a three-year-old, and I was diagnosed with cancer the same week. Literally, the first day on the job, I was diagnosed, and that was a real shot in the dark.

I had two options. At the time, I actually remember having thoughts of, "Quit, and crawl in a hole." Or, "Just do it."

My grandmother never told me that part about quit and crawl in a hole. So that wasn't an option. So I did what I think everybody does—get as much information as possible and try to figure out, "Okay, what do I have to do with Autodesk?"

I convinced my surgeons to wait a month, which they normally don't like to do, before surgery. So I waited a month, got a couple of management people in place, and told the company I'd be back in six weeks, which was faster than the surgeons said I should. That was probably stupid, looking back. At the time, it seemed like the right thing to do. I had the surgery, the chemotherapy, and just kept going.

I was running the company while doing chemotherapy. I believe that's a great focus. Between family and work, you don't have time to think about "Do I feel bad today?" or "What awful thing is happening to me?" And I just think the human spirit has great capacity if you just let it go. If you try and rein it in so it's too inward-focused, then all of us could go back to a fetal position.

I know everybody wants to hear that you sit by the ocean watching the waves roll in, but I didn't do that. I was—what, 42, 43 years old. I knew I was going to work longer. Yes, I had cancer, but I didn't think that had to be a death sentence; and so, I wanted to get more information about "How will I get through this?" and "What does it mean?"

I knew I had a couple of weeks of doctors to get that figured out. But I honestly never sat there and said, "I should quit." Maybe that's a weakness people who push so hard have, is that you don't know about the quitting part. You just say, "I signed up to do this; I'm really interested in this—I want to do this. And I'm going to do it. This other thing, I've got to get out of the way." I had a vision for what Autodesk could be, and this was a distraction.

I told the staff. But I also told them I'd be back, and I told them when I'd be back. I came back on that exact day.

I believe that they saw me being strong through the process. I got so many cards, banners, and flowers from the employees. And they were so clever because instead of everything coming the first week, literally, they had it all planned, department by department—it rolled out over, you know, a month. So it was every day— my daughter thought it was a big party because every day something would show up. And she just focused on the excitement of that. When I came back, they saw I was really dedicated, 'cause I think they knew I could have called it off, but that I wanted to be there, and that I was working through a tough time with chemo.

People who know me probably would like me to be a little less energetic. People who know me like me to chill out a little bit. In fact, one of my new VPs at the time said, "Oh, my God! If this is what she's like during chemotherapy [*laughs*], what comes next?" So I just refused to let that be an excuse for anybody around me or me.

When you become a CEO, you have to get some pretty thick skin. Every company goes through cycles. I don't care who they are. I don't care if they're HP, Apple, Sun—name your favorite company—there's a cycle involved. Good times become not so good; not so good become good again. You just don't know how long the cycle is, how deep it will be.

Just being an executive in a company toughens you up, but you're not tough until you're CEO. First of all, there's nobody to complain about. It was always easy to say, "You know, Ken did this," or "Scott did that," and "Gee, I would do it differently." All of a sudden, you're you, and you just have to toughen up. Any criticism— some of it's true, and some of it's just ill-placed. Whenever I get a little too upset, I say, "You know, they can come do it, and do it better, if they wish." I'm just a little calmer about it now.

Reset

What's happening in technology today is that everybody is back playing start-up. The whole Web adventure is a start-up. In fact, we have to admonish ourselves to be start-ups inside Autodesk, and we're doing that. I don't think I'd want to go to a 60,000-person company. I like being able to walk around and know a lot of the employees, and I like knowing the customers and our partners. But at the same time, scale gives you some opportunity.

My daughter turned 11 yesterday. Her dad gets a little irritated because when he starts to answer her questions, she says "No, Dad, Mom is an executive of a technology company, I'll ask her this question." [*Laughs.*]

I think you can stay too long as a CEO. I don't have a "too

long" in my mind quite yet, but I hope to not overstay. I've said many times to my staff, "Hey, we have an open shop here. So if you start thinking I'm getting crusty, bring it out."

I never have believed you should plan too hard about what comes next, because you miss everything that way. I didn't plan to be CEO of Autodesk; I didn't plan to come to the Valley; I didn't plan to go into computer science; I didn't plan any of these things. And I'm in such a wonderful place, why plan the next five years? There's something more exciting and bigger out there for me, my family, and my work life. I really believe that, and that's why I get up every day and get back out there and get shot at from all sides [*laughs*] —why not? As my grandmother said, "What else you got to do?"

Many of the jobs I took, I wasn't comfortable taking, because I thought, "Gee, am I really the best person?" So it made me try a little harder: I think it made me listen a little better. It made me rely on the folks around me and then we all got successful. I think you have to constantly jump out of your comfort zone into something that seems a little scary. If you do that enough, then you can take really big, scary things on, because you've practiced.

In the course of a story for *Forbes* ASAP, I drove with a reporter up to Autodesk a few months after the shoot. There, I was once again reminded of the role an entrepreneur's personality plays in the culture of his or her company.

On the day we arrived, there was a children's book sale taking place in the lobby. Employees, in casual—even ratty—clothes, walked back and forth, chatting happily. Some had their dogs with them. It looked like Paradise, Marin County style. We were escorted to the refreshments room, where we loaded up on bottled water and muffins, and then went into Bartz's office. Though the topics were different, the conversation over the next two hours was identical in tone to the one you've just read. Whether in front of the cameras or alone in her office, Carol Bartz is the same person. She feels no need to be anyone else.

Al Shugart
Founder, Shugart Associates and Seagate Technology
Founder, CEO, and Chairman, Al Shugart International

The Man
- Born on September 27, 1930
- Raised in southern California
- Earned a B.S. in engineering physics from University of Redlands in 1951
- Remarried, two children and three stepchildren

The Entrepreneur
- Founded Shugart Associates, a floppy disk manufacturer, in 1973; fired by board of directors in 1974
- Cofounded Seagate Technology, a disk drive manufacturer in 1979; fired by board of directors in 1998 (Seagate has since been acquired by Veritas Software)
- Founded Al Shugart International, a venture capital and public relations services firm in 1998

"I always thought that I enjoyed life more than everybody else. So it doesn't bother me if somebody drives by in a Mercedes and I'm in an old fishing boat. I'm sure that I was enjoying life more in my old fishing boat."

$\mathcal{A}$l Shugart has lived through what is the greatest nightmare of a successful entrepreneur: to drive past the headquarters of a successful company that you founded but no longer work for . . . and see your name still on the sign.

Shugart was already a legend in the computer disk memory industry, having made his mark at IBM in the early 1960s. But he really cemented his reputation by starting Shugart Associates, which in the early 1970s was among the world's leading floppy disk drive makers. That was where I first met him, a born iconoclast who reveled in being outspoken and unpredictable.

Perhaps a little too outspoken and unpredictable: In 1974, the board of Shugart Associates threw its namesake out the door. The company was never the same again, eventually being bought by Xerox.

As for Shugart, he said to hell with Silicon Valley and took off over the mountain to run a saloon and a fishing boat in Santa Cruz.

He loved the life, but anyone who knows him also knows that

Al Shugart wouldn't stay out of the Great Game for long. Sure enough, the next time I saw him, Shugart was wearing an uncharacteristic suit and sitting in a huge office at the headquarters of his new company, Seagate. Siting Seagate in the mountain town, Scott's Valley, Al had come halfway back to the Valley—just close enough to throw bombs.

Seagate grew to be a billion-dollar company, and once it bought its toughest competitor, Conor Peripherals, it became the single dominant player in PC hard disk drives. Now rich and vindicated, Shugart began to once again indulge his eccentricities. He backed various California state political propositions, ran his dog for office, and even returned to his saloon uniform of Hawaiian shirts. If entrepreneurs are driven by the need to order their world, then Shugart's vision of himself seemed to be the opinionated guy at the end of the bar.

Yet, for all of his snubbing of tradition and his outrageous public pronouncements, Al Shugart was as cagey and tough a businessman as Silicon Valley had ever known. That skill, however, didn't save him when the PC industry stumbled and, as a result, the disk drive business collapsed. Shugart found himself tossed out of the second great company that he had founded. At least this time it didn't bear his name.

These days Shugart is a venture capitalist, running a typically idiosyncratic little operation. As if in a gesture of truce to his old nemesis, he's headquartered the company in Silicon Valley. But he hasn't come all the way home: Shugart still lives 90 miles away from the Valley in Pebble Beach.

He arrived at the shoot wearing a loud tropical shirt and a devious smile. I knew I was in for another adventure with crazy Al.

I've had the entrepreneurial fervor since I was six years old. That was in Chino in southern California. I had a paper route, and, in fact, I published a newspaper from my house. I don't recall if I ever made any money on that. But later, I ran a little bicycle repair shop in my backyard, underneath the walnut tree.

I always was doing things like that. I didn't know we were poor at the time; I only found that out later. Then, I began wanting to make some contribution to the family by supporting myself, so I was constantly looking for things to do. I had several paper routes, and so forth.

I was brought up by my mother as a single parent. I never lived with my father. He was a structural engineer and he remarried, I guess, when I was probably three or four years old. I had a good relationship with him, but I never spent very much time with him. My mother raised me and my sister, who was five years older than me.

My mother was a wonderful woman. She was a great teacher. Actually she was real teacher: She taught elementary school. She had a good set of social values, which she passed along to me, and I think I got those very, very early.

She enjoyed life. I think she also passed that on to me. I learned very, very early, you have to enjoy life, and she was the one that taught me that there wasn't a shred of evidence that supports the notion that life is serious.

She also taught me to be socially responsible and be fiscally responsible. She used to say, "All work and no play makes Jack a dull boy," but then she added, "All play and no work makes Jack unemployed." She always added that.

In those days they didn't have Little League, but there was always a baseball game somewhere. I must have been 12 years old or so and I said, "Mom, I really played well today. I caught several fly balls, picked somebody off second base, and I hit a single and a triple. Wasn't I good?" And she said, "Alan, you were good. I just wish somebody else had told me." And I remembered that all my life. Nobody likes a braggart.

I probably wouldn't have gone to college if I had not gotten a scholarship to the University of Redlands. My father introduced me to an individual who had a scholarship set up at the Redlands, and I took the test and passed. If I had not been introduced to this fellow by my father, I probably wouldn't have gotten a college education.

Big Blues

IBM was a great learning experience for people. I started there in 1951 and left in '69. I was the radical, but nobody ever complained about that. I was also very much a company man. The only dress code that I ever broke at IBM, I think, is that my white shirts with ties were short-sleeved.

You can be an entrepreneur in a big company [like IBM]. Look at these little companies that are starting out. The person that starts one, you say, is the entrepreneur—I don't believe that. I think there's usually several entrepreneurs in those start-up companies. And I think I was allowed a lot of freedom at IBM. Did I learn to become an entrepreneur? I don't know what an entrepreneur is, but IBM fostered vision from its employees and the execution of vision.

An entrepreneur's a visionary, but a long-term visionary and a short-term visionary. He is somebody that has an idea and knows how to make it work and then continues to have ideas on that first idea. That's an entrepreneur. But you can have a lot of those kinds of people in the same company. That was IBM.

IBM does a great job of generating camaraderie with their employees and educating their employees. I think IBM is a great company.

Eventually, the company transferred me to New York from San Jose, and I didn't last very long. I'm just not your basic New York type, I guess, and I lasted about a month or so and then I turned in my resignation. They tried to keep me and offered me some big jobs, including a lab manager's job back in northern California, but by that time I'd already made up my mind to quit. I just went out by myself. I had no job.

After the word got around that I'd resigned from IBM, I got a telephone call from Larry Spitters at Memorex. He said, "I understand you don't want to work at IBM anymore; we'd like to talk to you about a job." I said, "Well, maybe in a few weeks," and he said, "I need to talk to you this week so you can start next Monday." *[Laughs.]* So I talked to Larry Spitters and Jim Guzzie and went to work at Memorex within a week. But I had no plans to work at Memorex when I quit IBM. I stayed at Memorex three and a half years. I started at Memorex in mid-'69 and left the first of 1973.

Why? In late '72, I thought Memorex was gonna miss payroll. If you'll remember, Memorex was doing very, very poorly. They'd started to get into the computer business and their financial situation was just looking terrible. I was concerned they were gonna miss a payroll, so I thought if somebody's not gonna pay me, it might as well be me.

I got several of my pals together and I said, "Why don't we go start our own company?" They said "Okay," and we did it. I was not dissatisfied with Memorex, only with the exception that I was afraid I wouldn't get paid.

A F l o p p y H i t

We started Shugart Associates with the objective to manufacture eight-inch floppy disk drives; the floppy disk drives were just taking off, and we thought that IBM very shortly would announce data entry devices that used floppy disks. Until then they were only using floppy disks as program load devices for computers and controllers.

So we started the company. Everybody kicked in a few thousand dollars; we didn't have very much. We probably could have lasted three months. But I got a hold of a friend of mine at Sprout Capital Group. I told him what we were trying to do and they funded us right from the beginning.

It was a very small amount because we weren't doing any manufacturing at the time. And I don't even remember what amount it was at all—maybe a few hundred thousand. And then after that we got a little more investment from Hambrecht & Quist, then a European company that invested in us, and a couple of others, I can't remember. We never took a lot of money in.

I've always thought you should have a good time. Life is not serious, and we were having a good time. We were doing some good, and we thought we'd be successful.

I was at Shugart Associates in 1973 and 1974, and within those two years we didn't expand very much. Then the board of directors and maybe a couple of executives didn't want me to be the CEO anymore. I got fired. Got fired from my own company.

Actually, I don't know if I got fired or if I quit. A friend told me later that, for a person in my position, the difference between firing and quitting is about five microseconds.

I recall driving by Shugart Associates and seeing my name on the front of the building. Not being there anymore was an emotional problem. Not emotional for me, but emotional in that I felt like I let down the employees by not being there and not doing the right kinds of things for them.

Casting Off

I decided to move to Santa Cruz.

I bought a house on a cliff overlooking the ocean—wonderful place, pool and everything. I joined a couple of other people and bought a bar. I really didn't run the bar, but I financed it. I worked a little bit at the bar, and my daughter, who was going to the University of California at Santa Cruz, also worked Sundays at the bar.

I had a good time. I bought a fishing boat and was fishing for salmon and albacore, and selling it. I love Santa Cruz. Much more so than Silicon Valley. I like the people. In fact, I like the Santa Cruz people better than I do the Monterey people. My home now is in Pebble Beach, but I'd rather be in Santa Cruz. It's just a great place.

My day started overlooking the ocean, hearing the water, and so forth. I didn't have to be at work at 8 o'clock in the morning, so therefore I could miss the traffic. I would go at 10 or I could go at 5.

I was also doing consulting. In fact, I did most of my consulting from home. I would consult for a while and, depending on the particular day, I might have to go to the bar and clean up from the previous night. Depending upon the season of fishing, I might go out very early in the morning and catch salmon. So all these parameters worked toward telling me what I should be doing that day.

I was fishing commercially for salmon or albacore later on in the year. I fished out of Santa Cruz or when the Santa Cruz harbor shoaled over I sometimes moved my boat to Moss Landing. One year I moved my boat to San Francisco and I berthed my boat in Bolina Bay, in Alameda. I fished every morning out of Bolina Bay.

The fishing out of San Francisco Bay was fantastic. You'll never have another experience like going underneath the Golden Gate Bridge in the morning and coming back at noon. It's just magnificent. It's just great. Particularly if you've caught some fish and you can stop at Alioto's Fish Market and sell it.

I always thought that I enjoyed life more than everybody else. So it doesn't bother me if somebody drives by in a Mercedes and I'm in an old fishing boat. I'm sure that I was enjoying life more in my old fishing boat.

I'm very fortunate. I didn't feel badly about myself during that

*Ukulele memories: Al Shugart, before he switched
from Hawaiian music to Hawaiian shirts.*

hiatus. I was enjoying myself every day. Thought I was always doing good for people and doing good for the world. I never felt sorry for myself.

I think about the bar and the fishing boat sometimes, but I don't miss 'em because they've been replaced by other endeavors.

Shugart Redux

I'd been divorced for 10 years or so, and in 1979 I remarried. I married the ultimate consumer, Rita. I'm still married to Rita. She's still the ultimate consumer. So I had to go back to work. That's why I started Seagate in 1979.

The disk drive business is tough. I really don't know why anybody would be in that kind of business. I would not want to go back into that kind of business, no question about it. But I never woke up at three o'clock in the morning worried about it.

It was a tough business in the '80s. There were too many PCs and not a big enough market for our disk drives. You could probably blame us for not looking ahead and seeing that it was going to happen.

We hit some tough financial times. I was running around to the banks in New York, looking for a loan. They kept sending me to the workout department, which is for all the deadbeat accounts. But I never had any doubt that we would get the money and return to profitability. I always had confidence that we would survive and we would get money and we would grow again.

During those times you have to deal with a number of problems. You're scrambling to get money, you're racing around trying to maintain relationships with people, and then you have layoffs.

Dealing with it—that's all part of being a leader, I guess. A leader has to be able to juggle a lot of balls and not drop any. It never occurred to me that I had an impossible task at all. It was just the job

at hand and I did it. Looking back upon those times, they were probably very educational, I imagine — I probably learned a lot.

Thrice Around

I got fired from Seagate in 1998. I'm not at liberty to talk about it
in great detail, but I think at the time what I said and what the
board told me was that it was time for a change. That was the only
reason I was given for being fired from Seagate. It was time for a
change.

So we formed Al Shugart International. We have eight or nine
employees. We're a start-up resource company. We'll look for start-
up companies that are looking for money or public relations or
employees or advice of any kind. We can help them for a price.
The price is usually equity in the company. We don't like the word
"angel" because we supply a lot more assistance than what the normal angel would supply.

The fundamental things that we're looking at when we look
at a start-up, whether we want to make an investment or get
involved in any form, are, number one, is it gonna be fun and
interesting? If the idea's not gonna be fun and/or interesting,
we're not gonna do it. Number two, do we like the people? The
people are very, very important. And then if those two things are
satisfied, then we'll look at the business economics. This is a lot
of fun — a lot of fun and we're doing some good. We're giving
some bright people the capability of becoming successful themselves. I like it.

We invest in things other than just high tech. In fact, one of
our investments is in a company called Orange Guard, located in
Carmel Valley. They make a nontoxic pesticide made out of
orange peels. So it's not just technology.

One of the things that Al Shugart International offers is that
gray-haired stuff. I'm able to give adult supervision to a lot of dif-

ferent little companies without having to be on their board. I'd like to see more of that. I'd like to see more wisdom involved in the industry somehow.

I really enjoyed success, and not just my success. I like to do things well. Doing things well in the disk drive business was very challenging, but we did things well. But I like other people's success, too, and so when I see all these kids starting companies and becoming billionaires, I'm happy for them. That's success. I like to see people successful. I think it's great.

Would I get involved in running another start-up myself? I don't rule it out. I have no plans to do it. I would be surprised if I ever did it again. But I learned a long time ago that you don't rule anything out.

A D a t o C u s s

I always have been an independent cuss. That's part of being an entrepreneur. The only two companies I've ever been fired from were the two companies I started. I didn't get fired from Memorex. I didn't get fired from IBM, which were the two other companies that I had worked for.

I think being independent is not black and white, either. There has to be balance. In order for you to operate well as an independent, you have to have a lot of real good employees or real good friends.

I have the Malaysian title of *dato*. It's analogous to being knighted in England. I'm a dato and supposedly I get special privileges for life. I think so far the biggest privilege that I've indulged in is being able to tell newspaper reporters I'm a dato.

But in Asia, it makes a difference. It's a significant thing to be a dato, particularly an American. Usually they're homegrown Malaysian people. A fellow used to pick me up at the airport in Panang and he could park in the red zone to pick me up because he would tell the office that he was there to pick up Dato Shugart.

Is entrepreneurism an inherited trait? Absolutely. It's a genetic thing. Absolutely genetic. I don't think anybody can teach entrepreneurship, like you can't teach leadership.

I went to the University of Redlands about four months ago to give a speech to the students, without realizing that the president of the university had previously talked to them about their new leadership training classes. I told all the students that leaders are born and not made. Oh, boy. But I believe entrepreneurs are the same way, they're born and not made. That doesn't mean because an entrepreneur is born they're automatically an entrepreneur, but that capability exists. Sometimes it stays dormant forever. But once entrepreneurship appears, it never does end.

I think the important thing that people have to have and practice is a set of social values. I think this is so important. Being ethical, honest, and fair is fundamentally important. Character really is a critical factor in being an entrepreneur. If not critical to get some venture capital, critical to be successful. Absolutely.

Hiring people is simple. One of the things I think that I've been very good at and still am good at is hiring good people. Always hire people that are smarter than you. There's only two rules: Are they smart, and do you like 'em? That's all there is. And if employers would just follow those two rules, they would always have good employees.

I always had people that worked for me that really were experts. So I get credit for a lot of inventions that I didn't invent, other people did.

Raising a Ruckus

If you're so tied up in your own company that you can't do anything else, then you're not having a good time and you're not gonna be contributing to society. You have to do other things. Balance is the key. You must really balance your life and do different kinds of things. You can't just focus in on exactly what you're doing at work and have that be your life. That's a real mistake.

Politics was one of the things that I got involved [in]. I got involved in other things, too. I'm a great lover of animals, and I became active in the SPCA at the same time.

I object to politics generally. But I've been involved on the periphery of politics for a long time, just because I think that citizens aren't active enough and ought to be more active. I ran my dog, Ernest, for Congress from the Monterey area in 1996 as a protest. The Friends of Ernest was a nonprofit corporation trying to provide a vehicle for protest and get more people to get active in politics.

I'm worried for my country. I don't think our country's managed very well. There's some very fundamental things that have to be changed very quickly. Like campaign finance reform. And the income tax thing is absolutely crazy. Why would anybody want to reduce the income tax 10 years from now right now when you don't know 10 years from now what your costs are gonna be? The other problem with the income tax is, it's too complicated. Let's figure out what we need and then figure out how we raise the money to pay for it. Our country is out of control from a management standpoint. That really, really bothers me.

I started the "None of the Above" campaign to have it put on the California ballot as an option. The whole idea, though, is to get more people to vote. Right now they protest in California by not voting. Well, that's crazy. I want to give somebody a sign to carry so they can protest by voting for "none of the above" and it will be counted, recorded, and reported in the paper.

I think I'm doing some good. If I didn't think I was doing some good, then I wouldn't like it. If the politicians don't like it, then I know I'm on the right track.

A couple months after the shoot I received a Christmas card showing Al Shugart surrounded by his staff. All were wearing Hawaiian shirts. In the center was the Dato himself, wearing the big grin of a man having the last laugh.

Photo by John Harding

Gordon Moore
Founder and Chairman Emeritus, Intel Corporation

The Man
- Born on January 3, 1929, in San Francisco, California
- Earned a B.S. in chemistry from the University of California at Berkeley and a Ph.D. in chemistry and physics from the California Institute of Technology
- Married, two children

The Entrepreneur
- Cofounded Fairchild Semiconductor, 1957
- Devised Moore's law in 1965
- Cofounded Intel in 1968 and built it into the world's leading semiconductor manufacturer
- Intel year 2000 revenues: $33.7 billion (fiscal year ending 12/31/00)

"I talk to a group of students at the Stanford Business School about once a year. It amazes me—everybody in the class wants to start their own company. I don't think any of them have an idea of what they want that company to do, they just want a company. I couldn't operate from that direction. I have to operate from an idea first and then set up something to pursue it."

$\mathcal{B}$ob Grove and I had just finished our morning shoot, and we were lounging in the control room, having a quick lunch before our distinguished next guest arrived. Ann McAdam was outside, keeping a watchful eye for the arriving limousine.

I was gnawing on an energy bar when I glanced out the smoked glass windows toward the studio and saw a figure standing in the dark behind one of the cameras, quietly talking with a cameraman.

"Oh my God," I yelled as I jumped out of my chair, almost choking. Grove spun and stared, "Oh, Jeez." "What?" asked a technician. Bob pointed, "Gordon's here."

We bolted out of the room.

It was a quintessential Gordon Moore moment. Dr. Moore, one of the original Traitorous Eight who had quit Shockley Semiconductor to form Fairchild Semiconductor, the mother firm of modern Silicon Valley. Who had been part of the team that built the first integrated circuit. Who cofounded Intel. And who first defined the eponymous law that has proven to be the most influential meter of the modern world.

Gordon Moore, at that moment the richest man in California, had simply driven his own car over to the studio, found his way in a side door, wandered into the studio, and was now talking about video camera technology with a young man who had no idea he was talking to the patriarch of the digital world.

After nearly 40 years of living in Silicon Valley and a quarter century of reporting on high tech, I've met most of its great men and women. Some were lions, many were foxes, a few were even snakes. But there has been only one Gordon Moore: brilliant, tough, deeply moral—and, that rarest of rarities, a successful man of both self-effacement and deep humility. He is the ultimate scientist/entrepreneur, as good as Silicon Valley has ever produced.

Literally. Because, alone among the pioneers of Silicon Valley, Moore is a native, raised just over the Santa Cruz mountains in the coastal village of Pescadero. Knowing that goes a long way to understanding Gordon Moore. He is, in fact, the last successful son of Old California, exhibiting that almost forgotten combination of earthiness and high-mindedness, hands-on pragmatism and a belief that he can change the world. He is man of immense power, wealth, and accomplishment, and he adamantly refuses to put on airs.

I've known Gordon Moore for a long time, during which time he alone has not seemed to change. He still sometimes gets tears in his eyes talking about his old business partner, Bob Noyce. And, as I experienced in the course of the interview, he still gets a twinkle in his eye when he's about to tease his host.

Sheriff's Son

My hometown is Pescadero. It's the only town I know of in California that's smaller now than it was 50 years ago. That's where I lived till I was 10 years old, then I moved all the way to Redwood City.

My father was a law enforcement officer. He was the entire law enforcement on the coast side of San Mateo County. He covered almost from San Francisco to Santa Cruz. Initially he was elected as a constable, then he became part of the sheriff's office. When we moved to Redwood City, he moved to the county seat and he was undersheriff, the highest nonelective office in the sheriff's department.

He was about six foot, a couple hundred pounds. He was big but not huge, but he had a way of approaching things where he seemed to be able to settle people down pretty well. If there were fights or anything, he had to run off at night and take care of them. I was young enough then that I didn't appreciate that there was any special risk associated with that. Really, there probably was. In those days, there weren't many shoot-outs. My father always carried a gun. I never knew of him going out anyplace without carrying a gun, actually. He would get called out to some of the farm labor camps and the like. There would be knife fights and he would go in there by himself to get these things settled down.

The area was a bunch of small rural communities connected by a railroad that went down the peninsula and a couple of highways. There were fruit trees all over. In fact, my wife's grandparents owned a fruit orchard in the middle of what is now San Jose. It was about the last island left there. It was finally condemned for a grammar school when there was no other property for them to take.

I set up a chemistry lab in the garage when I was young. Those were the days when you could order almost any chemicals you wanted by mail order. It was fantastic. The things you could buy then were really things you could have fun with.

In my home chemistry laboratory, I used to turn out small production quantities of nitroglycerin, which I converted into dynamite. I made some of the neatest firecrackers, and I still have all 10 fingers! Those were simpler times. If I had made the explosives today that I made in those days, I probably would get into trouble.

I was fired as a *Saturday Evening Post* salesman. I was selling door-to-door magazines. I didn't make it at that. I just found cold-calling on houses to sell magazines was not something I was cut out to do.

I was trained as a scientist. I got a good education in the California schools. I started out at San Jose State College in 1946, where I met my wife. I chose to go there because I could commute from Redwood City and didn't have to leave home. I went to San Jose State for a couple of years and then I transferred to Berkeley, where I received my bachelor's degree.

The one time my father tried to influence what I did was when I went off to graduate school. He wanted me to go to medical school instead, but I really didn't have any interest at all in being a medical doctor.

From there I went to Cal Tech in Pasadena for my Ph.D. I was 24 when I got my doctorate. I lucked out. I had a good thesis topic and a professor who didn't insist on keeping the students around for an especially long time. I used to claim I hadn't been east of Reno, Nevada, until I got out of graduate school; then I discovered Pasadena was east of Reno. But as far as out of the state, Reno was as far as I'd been.

Now, I live within about three miles of where I moved when I was 10 years old and where my parents lived till they died. I guess I didn't get very far.

Strange Attractor

It's hard to believe that at that time there were really no good technical jobs in California. I had to go east to find a job I thought was commensurate with the training I'd had.

I found a job working in the flight physics lab operated by Johns Hopkins for the navy. At that time it was their principal missile development laboratory, and they had a basic research group that let me continue to do things that were reasonably closely related to what I'd done for my thesis.

I found myself calculating the cost per word in the articles we were publishing and wondering if the taxpayer was getting his money's worth at something like $5 a word. And I wasn't sure how many people were reading the articles anyhow. So I thought I ought to get closer to something more practical, and, frankly, I wanted to get back to California. I enjoyed living in the east for a few years, but I really thought I liked it out here better. So I started looking around for jobs.

Hughes was hiring a lot of technical people, but to do different kinds of things than I was experienced in. There were a couple of petroleum companies that had research labs up here in the Bay Area, but those didn't appeal to me either.

One of the places I considered seriously was General Electric Company, which at that time had an outstanding research laboratory that was doing a lot of interesting things. I interviewed there and at that time they were interested in getting people into their nuclear program. I wasn't especially interested in that. I also interviewed in California at the Lawrence Livermore Laboratory. The development of bombs I really didn't find very attractive so I turned down their offer, but that turns out to be how I got in the semiconductor business.

William Shockley was one of the inventors of the transistor. He grew up in Palo Alto, California, and when he was setting up this company, he wanted to come back to where he grew up. Shockley got permission to go through General Electric's files of the people to whom they had made offers that had turned them down; that's where he got my name. He was just setting up his laboratory in Mountain View, California.

He thought he needed a chemist because they'd been useful at Bell Laboratories. So he gave me a call one evening. That was the beginning of my exposure to Shockley and to silicon.

I was his 18th employee. Bob Noyce arrived on Friday and I arrived the following Monday. He was employee 17 and I was employee number 18. I always wondered what would have happened if I'd driven cross-country faster and gotten in on Thursday.

Bob was the only one of the group that had significant semiconductor experience before Shockley. I hardly knew what silicon was. Bob had been working with Philco Electronics, which was one of the leading transistor companies at the time. So Bob came in with much more specific knowledge than us, and he was a fantastic guy in any case.

Shockley was successful in attracting a bunch of us, but he also was a very complex person and very hard for many people to work for. I don't think "tyrant" begins to encapsulate Shockley. He was a complex person. He was very competitive and even competed with the people that worked for him. My amateur diagnosis is [that] he was also paranoid, and he considered anything happening to be specifically aimed at ruining Shockley somehow or other. The combination was kind of devastating.

He tried to make us take lie detector tests for a very minor incident that happened in the laboratory. He decided he was going to make the entire staff take lie detector tests to find out who was guilty. *The Caine Mutiny* was popular at about that time and we saw the analogy between Queeg and Schockley, wondering if there were going to be four or eight palm trees there the next morning.

I really measure the thing that's become Silicon Valley from Shockley Semiconductor in 1956. There were earlier technology companies—Hewlett-Packard and Varian in particular—but they were more like established companies on the East Coast. They were stable and growing nicely. Shockley introduced some instability into the system. He was the strange attractor that created the chaos.

A group of us decided that we'd be much better off if we could take advantage of Shockley's tremendous technical capability without being subjected to his management approach. So we actually went around Shockley to Arnold Beckman from Beckman Instruments, who was financing the operation, to try to do something where Shockley would be moved aside as the manager of the operation but would remain as some kind of a consultant.

I guess we kind of overestimated our power. We had a few meetings with Beckman that were moving in that direction. We were thinking of something like getting Shockley a professorship at Stanford. That's when we discovered that eight young scientists would have a difficult time pushing a new Nobel laureate aside in the company he founded. Beckman, on the advice of someone that he got in contact with, decided that would wreck Shockley's career and essentially told us, "Look, Shockley's the boss, that's the way the world is." We felt we had burned our bridges badly.

Fairchildren

We figured at that moment we just had to leave. This group of eight of us liked working together, and we wondered if there was a company that would hire the whole group. One of the group, Gene Kleiner, wrote a letter to a friend of his father's at an investment banking firm in New York. He essentially said: There's a group of us that like working together, do you think there's a company that'd like to hire the whole group? The investment banking firm sent out two people to talk to us, a senior partner and a relatively young Harvard M.B.A., Art Rock, who is now famous as the dean of venture capitalists.

Venture capital really didn't exist in those days. But they came out, and they spent an evening talking with us and essentially said, "You don't want to look for a company. What you want to do is set up your own company, and we'll find financing." So we said, "Okay, that way we won't have to move." We all had houses in Silicon Valley—they were much less expensive in those days. At that moment, we became entrepreneurs. I describe myself as an accidental entrepreneur. It all happened as a matter of chance.

We had a tough time tracking down a sponsor. We identified every company we could think of that might want to start a semiconductor operation. Actually, we took the *Wall Street Journal* and went down, one by one, all the companies on the New York Stock

From left to right: *Gordon E. Moore, Sheldon Roberts,*
Eugene Kleiner, Robert Noyce, Victor Grinich, Julius Blank,
Jean A. Hoerni, and Jay T. Last.
Start-up: The Shockley "traitorous eight" soon
after they founded Fairchild.

Exchange. We identified something like 35 companies we thought might want to sponsor us. The investment banking firm went to all 35 and they all turned us down without even talking to any of us. They just decided it was something they couldn't do structurally.

Then, luckily, they ran into Sherman Fairchild, who introduced them to the then chairman of Fairchild Camera and Instrument. Well, Sherman really liked technology and he wanted to do aerial surveying. He had set up a camera company and airplane company for the cameras; he was a true entrepreneur.

The fact that his father was one of the founders of IBM probably didn't hurt. Sherman was the largest individual shareholder at IBM at that time. After the introduction, the executive vice president of Fairchild Camera and Instrument came out and visited with us and was willing to take a shot at it.

Once we got a commitment from Fairchild to support us, we went off and started doing things that were at least similar to what we'd been doing with Shockley, setting up a new operation from scratch. I'm not sure if Shockley ever forgave us for leaving.

We got into the right part of the technology, through the photolithographic printing of the circuits, the development of the integrated circuits, and so forth. We were batch-producing a whole wafer full of transistors at one time and then cutting them up individually. One of the group, Jean Hoerni, had come up with an idea that he stuck in his notebook that really improved the transistor structure, making what we now call a *planar* transistor. It made everything flat on the top surface and kept the sensitive areas covered with a layer of silicon oxide.

We used a printing process on the first transistors, but we only had to print two layers. His idea extended that and you had to print four. So we couldn't try his idea right away because the scheme we had come up with only let us make three layers, and we needed the fourth one. So it lay dormant for a couple of years. When we finally did make the planar transistor, it was a giant leap forward in the stability of transistors, but it was also the platform from which the integrated circuit could be developed.

The opportunity that we exposed was quite a bit bigger than the company was capable of satisfying, so there were a lot of other approaches that were available. Our people saw those opportunities and, since we were a young company, they started running off pursuing those opportunities, getting financing elsewhere. Venture capital was becoming professional at that time. The first venture capital partnerships existed so people were able to get financing to carry on these ideas and form Fairchild. Literally dozens of companies were set up to pursue opportunities that were developed initially at Fairchild.

The turnover rates were very high in those days. It gets pretty frustrating when you're losing your best people. I had several instances where close friends and employees decided they were going to spin off and do something that was either directly competitive or closely competitive to Fairchild. It was a nuisance, but we had relatively little to keep technical people. It was before the days when stock options were very broadly spread around. Some people had options, but they didn't extend to all the technical staff by any means.

Fairchild was really the source of the Silicon Valley explosion. It set this whole idea in motion that a few young engineers with some good ideas could take some money and go off and set up a new company. That was really the difference between Silicon Valley and other places. The Boston area had a lot of high-technology companies, but they tended to operate in the classical vertically integrated mode and they never had this tremendous fractionation that existed out here.

Intel

The entrepreneur bug bit me in 1968, again for negative reasons. *[Laughs.]* I'm not a positive entrepreneur.

Fairchild Camera and Instrument, by that time our parent company, had acquired Fairchild Semiconductor Corporation.

They got rid of two chief executive officers in a six-month period and were running the company with a three-man committee of the board of directors, who knew nothing of our business, while they were looking on the outside for a new CEO.

Bob Noyce was the logical internal candidate, and they were going to pass over him. That kind of ticked him off. I realized that if they brought in someone from the outside, things were going to change quite a bit. I was getting frustrated with the difficulty of transferring new technology, from the laboratory I was running, into the production part of the organization. When Bob said that he was interested in leaving, I said, "I'll go, too." We resigned and started looking about to see what opportunity we could really define that made sense to pursue.

Finding funding for Intel was ridiculously easy. First of all, 1968 was one of the peaks of venture capital availability. There was a lot of money around looking for deals. It was before the tax law change of 1969, which really shut a lot of that down.

We'd been sufficiently successful at Fairchild and we were fairly well known, so we again called Arthur Rock. By this time Art was located in San Francisco and had set up venture capital partnerships. We asked him if he'd raise the money for us that we needed to get started. Arthur took the afternoon to call a few of his friends and by evening had commitments for the $3 million we wanted.

Bob Noyce was a fantastic guy. You know, he was extremely bright, very broad ideas, and a born leader. Not a manager, a leader. Bob operated on the principle that if you suggested to people what the right thing to do would be, they'd be smart enough to pick it up and do it. You didn't have to worry about following up or anything like that.

He was one of these rare individuals that everybody liked the moment they met him. And you know, I worked very well with him. I complemented him a bit. I was a little more organized as a manager than he was, though not an awful lot more.

I had hired Andy Grove directly out of graduate school at Fairchild, and in a short period of time he'd worked his way up from a fresh Ph.D. to being assistant director of the laboratory. Andy had done a superb technical job at Fairchild. He ran the group that understood the physics of the very important silicon oxide/silicon interface that made today's transistors possible. He did a spectacular job that is really some of the seminal technical work in the industry. The technical community knew him well. By that time he'd written what was the textbook for many years on the physics of semiconductor devices.

Exodus

When I told him I was leaving, he said "I want to come along." I didn't discourage him, I'll have to admit. Andy, we thought initially, would end up as something like our chief technical guy. And he started out worrying about the operations, the setting up of the manufacturing and the engineering activities. But it turned out that he just loved the idea of assembling an organization and seeing how it worked. He got over his Ph.D. essentially and started worrying about management kinds of problems. His horizons expanded when he got to Intel. Looking at the whole operation, seeing what it took to set up manufacturing, Andy is extremely well organized. He was at the opposite end of the spectrum from Bob as far as managerial capabilities are concerned. He is an excellent manager. The three of us worked very well together.

I became the chief executive officer in '75 and Bob stayed around there for about another decade. He spent less and less of his time on Intel's inside business, and took on a larger role as a spokesperson for the industry. He was part of the group that set up the Semiconductor Industry Association, and he took on a lot of the trade issues in Washington. Dealing with Washington was something I was very happy to have him do because then I didn't have to go back there.

He did an excellent job at it. His personality fit that beautifully. So Bob did a variety of things that were important to the company, but became very much less involved with what was going on inside. I picked that part up. And then Andy joined. We were faced with making a tough decision about getting into the microprocessor business. We had been in the memory business from the beginning, and it was the first product area we pursued. We'd been quite successful in it, generally. But we had not done a good job for two generations and we'd lost our leadership position. We had made the R&D investment to jump ahead of the industry again at the one-megabit level—a million bits of memory in one chip. We developed the technology. We had the product. But now we were faced with the decision of investing $400 million in facilities to become a major player again. It was at a time when the memory industry was losing a significant amount of money. It looked like it was going to be overcapacity forever and, well, it was emotionally difficult. The numbers just stared us in the face. The chance of getting a return didn't look very good.

Now, deciding to go out of a major business like that means a whole lot of other things had to happen internally. There were literally thousands of people that had to be reemployed doing something else or let go. We hoped we could reemploy them.

We just couldn't see making that next investment, so we decided it was time to get out of the memory business—the D-RAM business in particular—and we did.

We were very fortunate that we had someplace else to go. The microprocessor, by that time, had been designed into personal computers, and personal computers were becoming a very important part of the whole electronics business. So we focused our capabilities completely on the microprocessor and things around it. It changed the nature of the company.

I think Bob Noyce and I would have been severely disappointed if Intel had been less successful than Fairchild had been. Once you've been through it and achieved a degree of success, to back off much from that would be a problem. Still, no one could have predicted how important these products were going to become in the economy and how highly they were going to be valued.

The Law of the Land

I'd taken on the job of writing an article for *Electronics* magazine projecting what was going to happen in the semiconductor device area over the next 10 years. It was the early days of integrated circuits, and, up until that time, integrated circuits had mostly gone into military equipment and the like, where their small size and other advantages were important. But they were highly priced.

What I could see from my position in the laboratory was that semiconductor devices were the way electronics were going to become cheap. That was the message I was trying to get across in that article. I just looked at the first few generations of integrated circuits and saw that the complexity had been doubling about every year. By that time we had something like 60 components on an integrated circuit in the laboratory. I extrapolated for 10 years, saying we'd go to 60,000 by 1975 at the same price. It turned out to be an amazingly precise prediction—a lot more precise than I ever imagined it would be. I was just trying to get the idea across that these complex circuits were going to make the cost of transistors and other components much cheaper.

I was embarrassed to have it called Moore's law for a long time, but I've gotten used to it. I'm willing to take credit for all of it, but all I really did was predict the increase in the complexity of integrated circuits and therefore the decrease in the cost.

It certainly has become a self-fulfilling prophecy in a very important sense in that, to be competitive in this industry, you have to go at least that fast. The pressure to try to get ahead of the curve that's called Moore's law really drives the industry to a considerable extent now. We'll see how long it lasts.

The Pursuit

You know, I'm not an entrepreneur to the point where the most important thing to me is to go out and do something new. I would be very reluctant to go out and say, "I'm an entrepreneur, now what am I gonna do?" I'm much more comfortable in a position where I see an opportunity and then pursue it.

We saw an opportunity in setting up Fairchild to complete Shockley's initial vision, which we had abandoned: to make a silicon transistor. At Intel, we saw an opportunity to make very complex circuits and change the leverage in the business—which we did, starting with memory, and then by moving into the microprocessor. If we hadn't seen those opportunities, I would have been very reluctant to just go out and set up a company.

I have been married now for 49 years. I'm still a beach kid at heart. Unfortunately, my wife can't do that so much anymore. She's gotten to the point where she doesn't go very easily to some of the more remote areas.

One of my brothers was killed just a month ago. He was on the ranch in Pescadero, where he'd been since he got out of the Army in 1946. He was running around in an all-terrain vehicle. Unfortunately, it tipped over into a ditch and fell on top of him. My other brother runs a machine tool distribution business. In fact, he's only a block up the road from this studio.

I've been fortunate in, frankly, making a lot of money in this business over the years. My biggest challenge now is figuring out how to use that to have the most impact. I think it's harder to give it away than it is to make it initially, if you want to do it carefully and be sure what you're doing makes sense.

Conservation is one of the areas we're working on. I have a close association with one conservation organization, Conservation International, who I think does an outstanding job in their field. Our goal is to preserve as much of the earth's biodiversity as we possibly can. But that's one organization, and it's not sufficient to take care of the entire problem. I have to invest in many good opportunities. It's awfully hard to find enough hours in a day to track down others that are equally valuable.

My only advice to others is, be in the right place at the right time. It's easy to say and it's hard to do. It's something I was very fortunate in, I think. You know, I lucked out by being close to a few of the major, really landmark changes in the electronics industry. Not everyone can have that, but there are sure a lot of opportunities out there still.

≋

Subsequent to our conversation, Dr. Moore retired as chairman of Intel Corporation, assuming the title of Chairman Emeritus. He continued his deep involvement in charitable activities, especially those related to the environment. In late 2000, he and his wife, Betty, donated $5 billion to create the Gordon E. and Betty I. Moore Foundation, one of the nation's largest philanthropic foundations.

The last time I saw him, he was at a costume party, dressed as a cowboy. The sheriff's son looked right at home.

Photo by John Harding

Scott McNealy
Cofounder, Chairman, and CEO, Sun Microsystems

The Man
- Born on November 13, 1954, in Columbus, Indiana
- Raised throughout the Midwest
- Earned a B.A. in economics from Harvard and an M.B.A. from Stanford
- Married, three children

The Entrepreneur
- Cofounded Sun in 1982 and built it into a leading provider of network management software and hardware
- Sun year 2000 revenues: $15.7 billion (fiscal year ending 6/30/00)

"There are a whole bunch of people who don't have the ability to contribute. I believe in the 80/20 rule or the 95/5 rule. If you're blessed with the ability to be educated, have a great mind and body that allow you to work hard, you really owe it to yourself to deliver."

$\mathcal{W}$e sometimes play a game at *Forbes ASAP*. It's called "What would they be if they weren't who they are?" That is, if a major figure wasn't running a giant technology company, if his or her life had taken a different trajectory, where would that person be?

Once, in the middle of the game, someone threw out the name of Scott McNealy, founder and chairman of computer giant Sun Microsystems. There was a momentary pause, then someone said, "Club pro, Rolling Meadows Golf Course." We all laughed.

McNealy is something of an anomaly among America's business titans (Sun is a $55 billion company). He is perceived as being neither sophisticated nor dangerous nor charismatic nor brilliant. Rather, he is seen as a big, fun-loving guy with a toothy grin, who somehow, when he's not playing golf or ice hockey, manages to stay atop one of the most successful companies on earth.

Obviously, there is more to the story than that. But digging beneath the public façade of Scott McNealy, the superannuated frat boy, is tougher than it looks. In the past, Scott was known for the occasional, often hilarious, outburst and the inopportune remark in the press; now, with billions of dollars hanging on his every word, there is a gigantic apparatus in place to make sure that the real Scott McNealy rarely gets out.

While doing this interview, we got a close-up look at that apparatus and its effect upon McNealy. With the exception of Bill Gates, another man cosseted by publicity filters, McNealy's interview was the last in the series, having taken five months to set up. Even then, we had to agree to leave the studio and shoot at Sun headquarters. Once we got there, we were told we'd have to set up in an open atrium at the center of the building—a miserable place to shoot for TV, with harsh sunlight and employees staring down from balconies above.

McNealy, all grin and first-tee handshake and snide comments, arrived 20 minutes late, to be told by a nervous handler what the interview was about. We sat down, with employees poised anxiously around us, to talk.

The first 20 minutes was chat. McNealy was clever, but he gave me nothing I couldn't have found in a press kit. But then, as we began to talk about what McNealy had lost with his success, the years he had spent away from the lab, the time he now missed with his children, the interview grew darker and much more personal.

≋

Sun Rise

When we started Sun, there were four 27-year-olds who were the founders. I had three years' business experience, which was more than the other three founders combined. The good news was, I didn't go to all my business school classes. So we weren't constrained or hampered in any way by conventional wisdom.

I was working at this little computer company and a buddy of mine from school, Vinod Khosla, had had a parting of ways with his previous start-up and was looking for something to do.

In school, I had never talked about starting my own company, but he had. He did. No way I was gonna. I'm too conservative. I'm not a risk taker. So he wanted to and he went off and did it, and I said, "More power to you."

But then he wanted to start another. So while I was still working at FMC, in our spare time at night we started a company called the Data Dump. It was rent a word processor by the hour. We used big, four-phase centralized processing units to do time-share in an office by the campus. We totally lost all of the investors' money, including some of our own. We each lost about $5,000 of our own money that we didn't have.

Finally, we started Sun together, and the way all that came about is Vinod ran into a guy at Stanford who had invented the Stanford University Network workstation, the SUN workstation. He had all kinds of people calling him up, saying, "I want one," but he couldn't build 'em. So Vinod met him and said, "Let's go start a company. I know we can build a market out of this." The big question was, could they make them? Vinod told him, "I have a buddy who can make UNIX computers by the boatload." And so he brought Andy Bechtolsheim over, and I showed him our factory.

Vinod and I went out to dinner and we were fine-dining at the time over a Big Mac, fries, and a large Coke. He asked me when I was quitting. I said, "What are you talking about? I'm making 32 grand a year, I got a great job at Onyx." And he said, "You can't back out on me now." I said, "What are you talking about, back out? You haven't offered me a job." He said, "You don't offer founders a job."

The next day I went in and quit and we started the company. We had a business plan; it was four pages and would have flunked at Stanford. Absolutely would have flunked.

We raised a little money—about $250,000—got the thing started. We incorporated February 24 and we were profitable in May.

I never had any doubts about Sun. There was just no question it was gonna happen. There was no way we were gonna be disappointed if it didn't work out. We had a saying at that point: If we're gonna jump in the pool, we're gonna do a belly smack and empty the pool out. If we're gonna go belly up, we're gonna just empty the pool out while we do it. So we took a big, huge swing at it.

I think the best-titled book in the world is *Accidental Empires*, 'cause I think anybody who says they thought it all through and had it all figured out is just pulling your leg.

We did $8.9 million the first year, we did $39 million the second year, $115 million the third year, $210 million the fourth year, $438 million the fifth, and a billion-something the sixth year.

Back then it was a pretty aggressive growth, but you know, Compaq started at the same time and they actually grew faster. SGI grew a little slower, but they were higher margins and more profitable. Compaq was lower margin but much faster growth.

The first six months I was helping to design the boxes, I was dialing up every vendor I could think up to come in and help us get the parts organized, get the parts ordered. We'd order the parts, I'd write out the purchase order, they'd walk off with the purchase order. The parts would show up in the back, I'd unbox 'em, I'd build the little container, build the shelf to put the container on, I would mark the container with the part number, I'd put the parts in the container, I'd go over to the computer and log in the new part number and build the bill of materials, print the bill of materials out, and do the accounting, and . . . I mean, that's how we started. I was an individual contributor. Then I started to manage while individually contributing, then I did mostly managing, with a little leading. Then I did mostly leading with a little managing, and now I do just basically bully-pulpit kind of leadership. I don't get to make many decisions. I don't have time; I don't have the expertise.

My firm belief is that Sun invested for the long term. We took our hits early, we didn't compromise, we didn't cut corners, we built our R&D, we built our own intellectual property, but we opened our interfaces and ran at lower margin. It made it much tougher. We gave a lot more of the company to get capital. We shared the success with our employees very aggressively to build loyalty. At 27, we figured we wanted a place to live and work and do stuff for a long, long time.

The company kind of grew into me. Vinod and I had a little argument about who was gonna be CEO and I said, "No, you be CEO." And he said, "You be CEO, you're more experienced." I said, "No, you've done more start-up stuff than I have." So we went back and forth, back and forth, and I just said, "Vinod, you be CEO, I'll be manufacturing manager," and that's really how we got started.

I wasn't the original CEO and I wasn't the start-up CEO, and, I tell you what, the company wouldn't have gotten started and wouldn't have gotten launched in the same trajectory if Vinod hadn't done it.

We were looking for a VP of marketing and the board decided they liked this person so much they made him president. They kind of told him he was in charge and told Vinod, you're still CEO, and created an untenable situation for both of them.

So about two years into the company, they asked both of them to leave and asked me to take over temporarily until we could find a real CEO.

We're about 15-plus years into that search, and every board meeting I ask the search committee, "How's it coming? You got any candidates?"

The real story is, they went in and asked my team, "Is Scott the right person temporarily?" They all said yes. Then they asked, "Is Scott the right person long term?" and it was an 11-to-nothing vote against. So we spent the summer getting the company going, getting it back to profitability, getting it ramped up. We secured about a $20 million investment from Kodak and the board found a new CEO. It turns out that Kodak didn't really want this new CEO and told us the deal was off. So when Kodak came in they interviewed all our folks and it was an 11-to-nothing vote saying we'd rather have Scott than the new CEO. Kodak went in to the board and said, "You can have the $20 million, if and only if we don't hire this new guy, you keep Scott on as CEO, and we have veto rights over anybody else you would hire in a CEO for the next five years." And the board said, "Okay, Scott, you're CEO if you want to be."

I went home and my mom and I talked about it. My mom, to this day, regrets [that] she said, "Go for it. Just do it for a couple years, and then let somebody else do it." She thinks I work too hard.

Changing Goals

When I was young. I wanted to be a fireman. By the time I was in college I wanted to be an eye surgeon. About 60 percent of the Harvard undergraduate class was premed so I thought there were many smart doctors, so I got involved in economics and decided I'd go to business school.

I didn't even know you could get an engineering degree when I went to Harvard. They're fairly liberal arts oriented, and nobody explained to me that you could actually be an engineer. I might have been one, but I liked economics. It's a social science; it deals with people and with the science of micro and macro economics.

Bill Raduchel was a pretty important influence. He was my first economics professor. I took Ec 10 for fun, and he was his section leader and he did a great job. I really, really enjoyed what he was teaching, and I ended up becoming an economics major. He was my thesis adviser when I wrote my thesis on antitrust.

In school, I like to say, I majored in golf. That's what I always say. But my goal, actually, by the time I got to college, was to figure out, especially business school, how to maximize grade point average per hour invested. I just figured—and, in fact, it's paid off pretty well—when the marginal rate of return on any particular activity starts to dip, move on to something else where you get a greater return. So, if you had to spend an extra 7x hours to get the A, that just doesn't make sense. You don't have time in real life to go do that. You don't have time in real life to do perfect at everything, and you'd better get a lot of things done.

In my senior year, I was focused on trying to make the NCAA championships in golf. I missed it by one swing. I hit one out of bounds coming down the end. I just kind of did a European Ryder Cup maneuver at the end.

When I was just out of school, I played pretty well in a couple of tournaments and played pretty well at some of the courses where the pros were playing. I thought, maybe I'll do it. My dad got me all set up with our pro to go play the Rabbit tour in Florida. I was all set to go do it and Rockwell promoted me, at the age of 22 or something, to a fairly senior job. I figured, I don't like to travel, so why do that and not really know if I'm gonna make it. I'm doing well here in business, I got a big raise, and so I just played amateur tournaments.

Tiger Woods came over to my house over Labor Day weekend and he hit a couple balls with my driver. I'm very glad I'm doing what I'm doing, 'cause I looked at it and after the second shot, I said, "You know, it's not the driver." *[Laughter.]* In other words, it ain't the arrow, it's the archer, and I figured it's pretty good that he's golfing and I'm working in business.

First Job

I graduated from Harvard and took a manufacturing job in a plant in Centralia, Illinois. It was my old hockey coach from when I was 12 who hired me.

It was a little bit of a culture shock. This was a factory out in the middle of nowhere, an hour and a half from anything bigger than a silo, out in the hinterlands of southern Illinois. I was working in a plastics plant where we molded plastic parts for Corvette hoods and camper tops.

Fiberglass and dust were everywhere. The temperature during my first summer would be 110 outside and about 130 in the plant. The first couple of weeks I was there they took about six or seven employees out on stretchers from heat exhaustion.

Photo for Sun Microsystems by Court Mast of Mast Photography, Inc.

*Penalty box: Scott McNealy takes a breather
during a corporate hockey game.*

People would cook their TV dinners on the presses as they go up and down. About 20 minutes before lunchtime, all of a sudden you'd see these TV dinners going up and down on these fiberglass presses.

The first three days, all they did was have me take a couple of the employees—kids who were there for summer jobs—and supervise them cleaning up the lot outside. I'd go out there and I was working with them and they weren't real happy.

I started working these kids pretty hard, and the second day one of the parents hauled me aside in the plant, practically grabbed my collar, and said, "Quit working my kid so hard."

My parents always told Roger [Penske, McNealy's first employer], "Work him to the bone," so it was kind of interesting to learn that, actually, parents didn't want their kids working hard. I thought that was kind of strange, but what the heck.

Well, about the fourth day into it one of the foremen got fired for coming in drunk, so they asked me, at the age of 21, to become foreman. So all of a sudden I was foreman for 13 what you might call lifers—their average age was 35 or 40. They had kids older than me and all of a sudden I'm their boss. It was quite an experience.

Well, I did that for three months and then they transferred me to Ashtabula, Ohio, which we affectionately referred to as the Mistake on the Lake. I worked in another fiberglass plant there, doing two jobs. At the 10-hour early morning shift I was foreman on the finishing line, and then in the afternoon shift, I'd schedule the plant.

We didn't have ERP [employee resource planning] systems back in the old days, and you just got a big, wide sheet of paper and did spreadsheets, by hand. This was pre-spreadsheets, so I would basically plan the production for the next day. And then I'd go home and pass out.

I ended up getting sick. I told my boss one day, "I don't feel well," and he said "You don't look well." I drove home from Ashtabula to Detroit that night and I got home 'bout 10 o'clock, and by 4 A.M., my mom took me in to the emergency room. I was just fundamentally exhausted, and it turned out I had mono that had degraded into hepatitis. They strapped an IV bag on me and tried to get me back on my feet. I had to take a week off and the bosses in Detroit moved me back to corporate. I became a sales engineer and then a sales rep for the next year and a half before I went back to school. That was the start of my career. I learned I need to pace myself and I needed to listen to my body a little more.

Then I went to Stanford Business School. Well, I went to at least half of the classes, but I was enrolled for two years. I tried to get into Harvard and Stanford Business Schools out of college and neither would take me.

I tried again a year later and neither would take me. My theory is that the business schools don't like to take people out of school 'cause they don't know if they're gonna be any good. They only like to take people who've proven they're going to be superstars so that they can give them a degree and take credit for everything that happens thereafter. That's why they keep track of you so hard after you leave.

After business school I went to FMC Corporation in Chicago. I spent one winter out there and decided that's not so good and fell in love with this gal who lived out in California and worked at the FMC tank plant. I told my boss, either you move me or I quit. I moved out to California, and two months later I quit anyhow. So the moral of the story is, don't listen to some young kid in love.

Silicon Valley

Bill Raduchel called me and he was buying computers at the time for McGraw-Hill from this little company called Onyx. It was the first company to put the UNIX operating system on a microprocessor.

I didn't know anything about computers. I knew a lot about manufacturing. So, the first day on the job at Onyx, I walked in and said, "What are all these big black things?" And they said, "Those are disk drives. Big old eight-inch Winchester disk drives."

I asked, "Why are these little red tags on 'em?" and they said, "These are defects and we haven't gotten around to them." I asked, "How much do they cost?" and I looked and there was about $4 million worth of inventory on the side wall. The tags said NTF—No Trouble Found. I asked how they tested 'em over at our sister company and I was told, "They just build 'em and ship 'em over here."

I suggested we take one of our computers over there, have 'em plug 'em into our computer, and if they don't work, don't bother sending them over.

They thought that was a good idea. So we sent 'em all back, put a computer over there, and all of a sudden we generated about $4 million in cash by putting test procedures at their factory. We wrote up specifications on what the disk drive ought to do before they were allowed to ship it over. I didn't need to be a rocket scientist to figure that one out.

This was just so brain-dead logical that it's kind of like learning to breathe, you know?

Growing Up

I grew up all over the Midwest—Indiana, Illinois, Wisconsin, Kansas. My dad was with American Motors. He started off in purchasing and then in marketing and then became vice chairman. Not bad for a Harvard Business School grad.

My parents are very different. My mom's a homemaker and an interior designer—very outgoing, personable, and makes friends with everybody on the planet. Dad's very focused, very logical, and a very good businessman.

In school I was on the hockey team, I was on the golf team, I was on the swim team, I was on the baseball team—I played a lot of sports. I was interested in my father's work, and when he came home I would read along with him and see what notes he'd write. It was just fun to talk to him about his work. He'd be barbecuing and I'd ask him what he was doing at work.

I worked during the summers for Roger Penske. I started in his Chevrolet dealership, washing cars on the new car wash rack for a buck-seventy-five an hour. I worked my butt off and finally I got them to give me a raise to two dollars an hour at the end of the summer. It was pretty tough duty. I washed cars and parked cars— I did every job in a car dealership you could imagine.

During the weekends I would go out with his Goodyear race tire team on a truck and we'd drive out to the races. I'd be in the pit crew changing rubber to wheel and then they'd roll the wheels off to the pits and change 'em on the car. We were back there just covered in tire soot and mud, basically airing and balancing the tires.

I did that for three-and-a-half bucks an hour. That was big money, let me tell you, and with Roger Penske you worked hard. I used to be on overtime Wednesday afternoon and that was before I went to the races. I was working 90 hours a week for Roger.

I was always sure I'd have my own business. Having grown up in Detroit, I knew when I was 40 or 50 I would have saved enough money to start a tool-and-die shop of my own and maybe have 30 or 50 people working for me. That doesn't sound bad right now.

Corporate Culture

I left on the day before April Fool's Day and I came in one day and the staff had carpeted my entire office with actual sod. There was a water hazard, there was a green, an elevated tee, a bench, a ball washer, and a golf cart. So I played golf for most of the morning. I was driving around in a cart. I took out a couple of cubicles and knocked a couple tables over in the cafeteria; it was fun.

My comments about Bill Gates are all theater. They are meant to be funny. Most CEOs aren't hilarious, that's their problem. People want to write about it. And if they're gonna write about Gates, I'd like to be in the article so it's a wonderful thing. Press is free.

My PR people tell me all the time not to say things. I can't help myself. I sat through so many speeches and presentations and classes where the professor or the speaker was boring. It was like somebody was sticking a poker in my eye, it was so boring. It hurt. So I always go up and try and be at least three parts entertaining and seven parts content. It's stuff that's funny; it's stuff that's true. So when I say stuff, it's usually got a really strong hint of truth, and that's why people laugh at it.

Now

I don't do politics, I just—I do company. I have a job. I got elected by, not the citizens, but rather by the shareholders, and I feel that's my number one responsibility professionally. I've got a lot to do at home with a wife and three little boys in car seats. So I have plenty to do.

Balancing being a CEO of a corporation and having three little kids at home is hard. Sleep is just kind of on the back burner. I sleep in airplanes. My wife's very good—she puts a pile of pictures in my briefcase every time I leave so I always have pictures of them.

It was more fun in the old days, but this is more satisfying. I flew back from Florida last night and got in at about 2:30, did e-mail 'til 4:30, and was up at 6:30, and, you know, those bags under my eyes are real. Is that fun? No, it's not fun. Is it rewarding? It absolutely is. You meet with shareholders; you meet with employees who tell you about how they put their kids through school or they bought their parents a new home. There's nothing more rewarding than that. That's pretty cool.

Balancing it all is impossible. I don't spend enough time at the office, I don't spend enough time at home, but you just do the best you can.

I don't know anybody that's balanced. I tell my employees this all the time in our town hall meetings. I look at 'em and I say, "Listen, this is the most intelligent, capable, bright, experienced, well-educated, just flat-out capable group of folks on the planet. You have a curse—you're cursed with the ability to work very hard, very productively, and very effectively. You have no choice but to exercise and live within that curse and do a great job."

With Scott McNealy's admission that he could not reconcile the demands of his professional and private life, the interview abruptly ended. Claiming we had run out the clock and that McNealy had other pressing appointments, the Sun PR lady stormed onto the set and announced that the interview was over. The real Scott McNealy had momentarily emerged, blinking and sad, into the bright sunlight . . . and had been quickly shoved back into the box.

"Thanks," was all he had time to say before he was whisked out of his chair, unmiked, his face wiped off, and led away, all while an assistant read to him a briefing document about his next scheduled meeting. As the phalanx marched off, I found myself thinking that Scott McNealy looked like a schoolboy on permanent detention—and pondering once again the costs of great success.

Photo by John Harding

Candice Carpenter
Cofounder and Former CEO, iVillage.com

The Woman
- Born on April 29, 1952
- Grew up in Ponte Vedra Beach, Florida
- Earned a B.S. in biology from Stanford and an M.B.A. from Harvard
- Married, two children (now Candice Carpenter Olson)

The Entrepreneur
- Cofounded iVillage.com in 1994
- Formerly president of Time-Life Video and Television and vice president of consumer marketing at American Express
- Currently managing director of Transitions Institute
- iVillage.com year 2000 revenues: $76.4 million (fiscal year ending 12/31/00)

"I think women are at a very amazing point in history where we've gotten everything we've ever wanted, and it may kill us, and we're trying to figure out how to manage it and live through it and in a happy way.

"Women initially were sort of following in the footsteps of men—this is the path to be successful. Then we all realized men are already over this. We're kind of following the wrong trail. Women were very focused for a long time, as I was, on how big is my salary, how big is my title. Then I thought the joke was on me because I ought to be wondering about what have I built in the world and how free am I to do what I want."

Candice Carpenter was an apparition.

Betting It All being a series about high-tech entrepreneurs, it naturally skewed toward the west, particularly toward Silicon Valley. Even the non-Valleyites such as Nolan Bushnell and Bob Metcalfe had spent most of their careers there; Virginia's John Sidgmore was more like a close cousin than a stranger.

But Carpenter was something else. Though she went to Stanford and spent years in Colorado, she was unmistakably a product of the East Coast media world. She had made her name not in chips or software but in publishing and television. And she had come up not through the labs or field sales but through powerful mentors. And whereas her female counterparts on the series, Carol Bartz and Kim Polese, were engineers and programmers at heart, it was obvious that Carpenter had never written a line of code in her life.

That made her an intriguing, almost alien, presence on the show—a fact reinforced by her arrival, looking stunning in an elegantly embroidered blouse and bringing with her an air of high-pitched Manhattan intensity.

To me, Candice Carpenter was more than just an object of curiosity, she was an interesting test of my theories about entrepreneurship. In many ways she was the antithesis of everything I thought of as a high-tech entrepreneur. Even more than that, she was the sole representative in the series of a new generation: the dot-com entrepreneurs.

As such, she was doubly intriguing—after all, as we were shooting, the e-commerce boom was in full swing, and it looked as though Carpenter and her peers would soon be both billionaires and masters of the universe. In early 2000, Carpenter's own company, iVillage.com, had a market valuation of $657 million—and her own net worth was more than $25 million. Were she and her dot-com counterparts really worth that much after only months of work?

Probably not, as the subsequent market crash showed. iVillage.com was one of the earliest casualties of the bust. Yet, unlike thousands of other Web content providers, iVillage.com is still there, still talking daily to millions of women around the world. Like Candice Carpenter, it is a survivor.

I got a glimpse that day in the studio of why Carpenter reached the pinnacle in her profession, not to mention a clue as to why iVillage.com would survive even the toughest times. Anyone who could cold-call the likes of Barry Diller or David Geffen and land a job is both brave and very sure of her abilities. So is someone who can run an Internet company while publicly professing that she hates computers and barely knows how to use one. But I'm most haunted by the image of this smart, talented woman throwing up before every important meeting of her life—a graphic image of real corporate courage.

Like anyone in the media business, Carpenter was careful and savvy in front of the camera. If the interview wasn't particularly warm, it was insightful . . . and I came away realizing that Candice Carpenter, for all the surface differences, was no different from her

West Coast counterparts. She, too, had been willing to bet everything on success.

Backwater

I grew up in Ponte Vedra, Florida, a little backwater place, but it
was actually a pretty good childhood. When I was young I was selling embroidered pillowcases to the neighbors and I was starting little cafes and all of that stuff.

My father was a shoe salesman and my mother was a very frustrated housewife who should have been Katharine Graham. She
was a really talented woman who ultimately started a newspaper. It
was very successful, but it wasn't the *Washington Post*. Had she
been let loose at an early age, she would have created the *Washington Post*.

One thing about my childhood that I think contributed a lot
was that I grew up on the ocean. It was back in the days when, literally at age four, I was allowed to wander up and down the ocean
all by myself because every neighbor knew us. I think that sense of
unboundedness actually has been with me and my choices my
whole life.

Outward Bound

I went to Stanford as an undergraduate. My major was really everything we've learned in the sciences, and how it applies. All the best
teachers there seemed to be teaching in their deep discipline, and
they decided to put together a course for people who would be citizens in the next century.

It's actually one of the best things I've ever done because I
became literate in all the sciences—not at the level of an experi-

ment in chemistry, but at the level of how is science done, what does it mean, and what's going on in all the disciplines collectively. It turned out to be great.

After graduating, I went to the mountains for seven years and I taught mountaineering with Outward Bound. I led kids in the mountains for five weeks at a time. That was a case of going my own way. I have always, more or less, gone my own way. All my friends were filling out applications to medical school and law school and I just thought, this is not going to happen here.

I was in Colorado and Wyoming, beautiful country. Probably the best training I ever could have gotten for the Internet. I just didn't know it.

In the mountains, what you end up doing is making decisions with very little information that are very important decisions with big consequences. You have to make them really quickly, you have no idea, and you develop your instincts.

You have to decide: Do I get these 20 people over the pass with the storm coming in, or do I not? Do I go for it or not? And, of course, you really don't even know what the weather looks like on the other side. So I got really comfortable making tough decisions and making them quickly. I think, in the Internet, that's turned out to be a very important skill.

I spent a lot of time by myself in the Grand Canyon and Canyonlands, but, honestly, being in the mountains with people is a lot more interesting. You learn an unbelievable amount about leadership and people in the mountains because people are themselves in the mountains after about three days. You see the real item.

A lot of people that I worked with at Outward Bound were on their way eventually to medical school or law school or business school. There were some long-term mountain men, but I didn't really see myself as a totally crunchy-granola person long term.

I felt like the bear who wanted to go up the mountain to see what was on the other side. I really didn't know what I wanted to do. I wanted to either be a psychiatrist to CEOs or go to business school. So I called the five top psychiatrists to CEOs and they all said, "You'll have much more fun if you go to business school and run a company." I said, "Fine. If you guys think so, you're the best guys in the field," so I went to business school.

After seven years of being in the outdoors, I went to Harvard for my M.B.A. At Harvard you specialize in believing you're going to be a CEO. *[Laughs.]* That's really what you learn.

I knew I was going to get through Harvard. The culture shock, though, was tough. I'd been in an environment where people just naturally took care of each other, and that's not necessarily what I found when I hit the East Coast establishment head on.

That's okay; I needed to make entry at some point. I think what I learned is so intangible. I actually think it really reinforced the idea of leadership, that I would be a leader. I was chosen as a leader by my class and by the faculty. I think it just reinforced that I had some real leadership ability that I could develop in whatever way I wanted.

Late   Bloomer

I was 31 when I got my first real job in the real world. I'm a pretty late bloomer in general.

My first position was with American Express, which is pretty conservative. I briefly considered Apple, which would have been a great fit, but I ended up at American Express. I had no idea what to do. I didn't have any context for the business world.

I consider American Express my boot camp in business. It's a very straitlaced culture, very serious, and very methodical. It was very slow and protecting of a great brand. What I learned is that branding just gets in your blood. From then on, for the rest of your life, if you have a brand and someone is doing something in your company that's not on brand center, your hair stands up on end.

You develop this tremendous sensitivity to what it means to be a brand. That was worth the six years I spent there. But I was not serious enough for American Express temperamentally, and that

*Society page: Candice Carpenter poses
near her childhood Florida home.*

was the problem. I thought I would like to actually be a little more myself. So I went to Time Warner, which is closer to my liking, more the media space.

I did some great miniseries with them. I got an Emmy from our first series that we developed, *Lost Civilizations*. It was great. It was shot in 40 countries and [was] really a tremendous series. When we won the Emmy, we were up against Ted Turner, so we were very excited.

Time Warner gave me profit-and-loss control over the unit. I was obsessed with that. I wanted the whole business. That's what I wanted to learn how to do.

I built a really good little company there. It was the first time I was really in charge, and it was really good experience. Time Warner gives people tremendous latitude to develop and to grow. And it was fantastic.

When I got to American Express, I didn't really care what job I took because the only job I really cared about was being able to run the whole business. I finally got to do that at Time Warner, and I loved it.

Meeting the Moguls

The business was going so well, and so, of course, I was completely restless. I went on a little journey. I wrote a lot of moguls: David Geffen, Barry Diller. They all called me, and I went to see them all.

I was working for people who were corporate people—they were not founders. And I was very interested [in] seeing what it looked like if you made something from scratch like Geffen and Diller had done—what does that look like? I walked in and their personal space looked completely different than anything I was used to.

Barry was working out of his home in this beautiful office, and Geffen had this kind of gorgeous space. Everything about them was different in a way that I thought was much more me.

This was much more being a brand that you carry around inside of yourself instead of attaching yourself to a brand. It was really the idea that captured me.

Diller is a genius, and he has a tremendous amount of integrity in a lot of unexpected ways. He's a man who really follows his own internal gyroscope, which I have come to tremendously respect.

Diller offered me a job at QVC (the Home Shopping Network), and in a way it was a kind of halfway house between the corporate world and my own. I learned a lot from him that I wouldn't have learned without working for an owner.

I learned that you don't throw money at something until you know you've got something. You let the market speak to you a little before you spend the big bucks on it.

I always said, "I work for Mr. Diller." I felt that was a brand I could align myself with, but I never said QVC, although I think he was pretty smart to go chase that direction.

I was with QVC2 (the high-end market of QVC) for about two years. It was long. Barry really is really annoying to work for, but he was like my halfway house between corporate life and building something. Every career has its little moments.

To Take on iVillage.com

QVC2 blew up because Barry got bought out. It just blew up overnight, which is the best thing that ever happened to me because it landed me in a place of no job and some money to think about what I wanted to do.

I mostly didn't want a job. That was my main motivation. I didn't want a real job at all. I didn't want a safe harbor. I had a one-year-old at home, and any sane person would have gone for security and the big paycheck.

In fact, I interviewed for a lot of big jobs like the ones I had, and always, on the way out, I'd go throw up in the bathroom. I thought, "I guess that's over. I'm not going to be able to do a big corporate job right now." It was something very visceral in me. It was like, "That chapter's over." It may come around again, but it was over for then.

I was very jealous of all my friends who had started the big cable networks—MTV and Discovery. I thought at the time, "The next one, I'm going to be there." I ended up doing some consulting for AOL because they told me I could come on a day-at-a-time basis. *[Laughs.]*

I was doing some work for Discovery Network, so I was having a pretty good time, actually; it was not a lot of responsibility on my shoulders. And I worked with AOL on the transition of their business model to commerce and advertising.

I remember, the day I thought working at home is not for me, I was going nuts. I was going crazy.

First Buy a Computer, Then Start a Company

I hate computers. I didn't have a computer until about two days before I came up with the idea for iVillage.com. I got a computer in January, had the idea for iVillage.com in April, and started it in June.

I knew there was a group out there that didn't even like their computers and really only wanted to know, what is this going to do for my life? And that was our idea for the site.

My team and I went to Kleiner Perkins, the venture capitalists. They really liked us, but we didn't quite fit in their model. They got all excited, but then they didn't quite know what to do—it didn't quite fit.

We basically said, "We're not taking no for an answer." We were very determined. Eventually they came in on the deal, and they've been phenomenal. I can't imagine not having them as partners.

I did learn something about raising money. I thought raising money was sort of like asking for something. Then I realized that the relationship between a venture capitalist and a company is a necessary relationship. They need us as much as we need them.

I don't know why this happened, but when we started going to see venture capitalists, we started eating steak, like there was some testosterone thing going on. *[Laughs.]* I don't know what it was— we just went on this big steak sandwich thing for that whole period.

With an adopted one-year-old in the house and starting a company, managing both was difficult. I did nothing else. Nothing else. I did not go out to dinner. I did not go on a date. I did nothing else. I did those two things, I think, reasonably well. I was just so exhausted by the end of it, I didn't wear makeup, I didn't have my hair done, I was fried, to be very honest. So then I adopted another child just to make life more interesting.

I would definitely tell anybody who's not prepared to sign your life away for a couple of years for a child, just don't go there.

When I first started the network for women, sisterhood was not the biggest thing in my life. But it is now. Women really experience and process differently, and people aren't afraid to say that now. One of the things I noticed is, when we had a lot of women initially helping to build the company, we would walk into the office, talk about kids and where did you get your hair done, how's the strategy coming. We'd cover the whole map of topics all in 30 seconds, no boundaries between these topics, intimacy to solutions.

Women can cross boundaries and topics really fascinatingly. If you give them a conversation, they'll cover the whole map in about 10 minutes. The network allows them to manage their stock portfolio, get help with their child, talk about their relationship and their marriage, and decide if they want to start a company, all in the course of half an hour. That is sort of how women operate.

Kick Ass

I have noticed that, once a founder creates a culture, the culture is set. Like if I wanted to change the culture, I would have a difficult time changing it because it's such a reflection of what we've put in place at the very beginning. I came out of corporate life where we had resources, we had scale—I actually liked that stage of the company. The start-up stage—personally, I don't know if I would do that again.

I think people with families are very appealing in terms of knowing they're going to have some balance and their priorities straight. So in many ways, I think being a mother or a parent just generally requires that you stay very grounded. It humanizes people and it makes them, you know, gentler, more compassionate, understanding to what the rest of the world's going through. If I had a really high-strung executive, I would tell her [to] go have a couple of kids.

One thing I have noticed is, a company is a lot more interesting when it's something you've built. When you really believe in it and you feel that it's making the world a better place for millions of women. I have to say that's pretty satisfying. My normal restlessness would have already kicked in, but when I get a little tired, now I go shopping for a few days.

Having children started with my passion for children. I'd have 10 children if I could. I don't think I started in time. I don't want to be blasé about being a working mother. I think women have liberated themselves, and now we have to kind of liberate the family. The whole family has to be winners. I don't know if we're quite there yet. I think that our culture has some work to do in making sure that kids don't get the short end of the stick. So I'm very committed to that issue and how we can help.

I think I'd like to be a minister at some point. I've always wanted to go to Yale Divinity School to be a minister and figure out what it would mean to be a minister now.

I'd also like to start a school that would be about producing kick-ass girls. Just completely kick-ass, amazing, compassionate, spiritually grounded, intellectually unbelievable girls.

I have a lot of things I want to do, so hopefully I'll live to be 150.

≋

I haven't seen Candice Carpenter since the interview. Her company, iVillage.com, soldiers on, but she has left the field. Her glamorous image occasionally appears in the pages of celebrities standing with other glitterati at some opening or charity event. These days she attends as an author: The title of her new book, *Chapters—Creating a Life of Exhilaration and Accomplishment in the Face of Change,* could also serve for her autobiography. I can even imagine the cover image of such a memoir: a little girl walking an empty Florida beach, determinedly dreaming about how she will make her mark in the world.

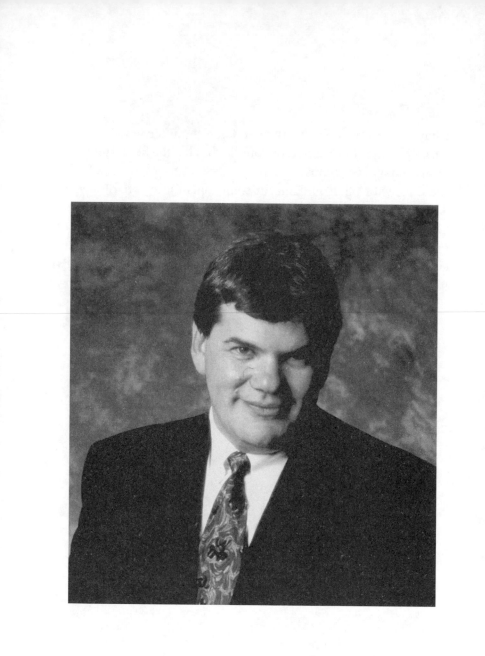

Philippe Kahn
Cofounder and CEO, Starfish
Cofounder, Chairman, and CEO, Lightsurf

The Man
- Born in 1952, in Paris, France
- Graduate and postgraduate work in mathematics
- Remarried, four children

The Entrepreneur
- Cofounded Starfish in 1994 after resigning from Borland (Inprise), a company he started in 1982 (Starfish has since been bought by Motorola)
- Cofounded Lightsurf Technologies (a wireless digital media company) in 1998

"I think that's a very entrepreneurial thing, always being able to focus on the next thing. It's something you learn from any competitive sport. Sailing is like that. You do a race and the race lasts an hour and a half. It's full of drama, but the next race is nothing to do with the first race and you got to be able to say, hey, it's over. Next race, and focus on the next opportunity. And it's hard but you learn how to do that."

$\mathcal{T}$ hough we'd crossed paths only a few times, Philippe Kahn was one of those people I'd learned to dislike from afar. Kahn ran Borland, an early software contender with Microsoft, based in the Santa Cruz Mountains just across the highway from Al Shugart's Seagate. A Frenchman turned California beach boy, Kahn was loud, arrogant, and publicity-hungry. For two Christmases, he sent me (along with everyone else in the electronics press) a CD of himself playing with veteran jazz musicians.

How transparent and pompous, I would think, tossing the disk on the shelf—a rich guy buying his chops. I made it a rule to steer clear of Borland whenever possible. But then Philippe Kahn surprised me.

Like every other company that went up against Microsoft in the early 1990s, Borland was slowly crushed by the Redmond Steamroller. I had expected, given his record, that Kahn would fume and despair publicly as his creation was ground into oblivion. Instead, he put up a good fight to the bitter end, accepted the end with dignity, and then disappeared. Clearly, he was not the man I thought he was.

We might have passed over Kahn as a guest for *Betting It All* had not his name unexpectedly popped up in the press just as we were putting together our guest list. It seems that Kahn, his name almost forgotten in the noise and excitement of the dot-com boom, was coming back into the game with his own Web projects. Ann McAdam found him, despite the disaster of Borland, more than willing to come on and talk about his life. In the face of all that had happened, the old Philippe Kahn had not been completely extinguished.

Like Shugart before him, he arrived at the studio in a barely buttoned tropical shirt (was this a mountain fashion fad?). Kahn was also busily stuffing a banana into his mouth—and when McAdam stepped up to introduce herself, Kahn, barely able to talk, took the wadded banana skin in his hand, threw it into a nearby trash can, then thrust out a still slimy hand to her. McAdam winced slightly and took it.

During the interview, Kahn proved to be a pleasant and entertaining subject. He was impressively forthright in talking about both his victories and his losses. Having won and lost fame and fortunes, he seemed a man with few illusions. At the same time, he also seemed, for good and ill, the purest kind of entrepreneur: brilliant, undomesticated, unafraid of either great success or failure and humiliation. Win or lose, he is going to play the game right until the last card is turned. And whether he is living in a mansion or his car by then, he will be happy for having been so long at the table.

I actually got married pretty young, I was 21; I had two kids when I came to America. I came first and they stayed in France until I could afford to bring them over nine months later.

When I started Borland, I worked for four or five years on this expired tourist visa. I didn't pay attention to it. I never left the country and never went back anywhere. I just built the business, until one day INS showed up. You get so busy that you forget. You really don't have time for that—I mean, that's a minor detail.

We had lawyers talking, and I was about to be deported. It was a complex situation, but eventually we made a deal. The punishment was that I had to go back to Paris to get my green card and spend a week there. I hadn't been out of the country, back to Paris where I grew up, for five years. So it was an opportunity, but that was the punishment. At the end of the day I got my green card and eventually became a U.S. citizen.

Cabinetmakers and Engineers

I grew up in Paris. My father was German, and my mother was French. On my mom's side, her family were Russian Jews who had been chased out in 1905. They were cabinetmakers, and instead of going all the way to America like *Fiddler on the Roof*, they stopped in Paris and stayed making cabinets there.

Now on my dad's side, his family were engineers for generations. They were German, those kind of German-integrated Jews who actually were part of Germany, and actually fought on Germany's side in World War I. Then they were really surprised to see that Hitler didn't like them anymore. So in the same way, they fled Germany and my dad joined in the French Foreign Legion to fight the Germans and was actually in an American uniform on D day.

My mom came from the French Resistance side and my dad came from the having fought in many uniforms on the Allied side. My parents met and then settled in Paris after the war. It's the perfect story. I was born in '52 and the story lasted until '59, when they divorced. My dad was quite a ladies' man.

They both passed away. My mom passed away when I was 13 years old and my dad passed away actually last year.

After their divorce, I lived with my mom, who was a professional person. She always had a job and she worked, so I spent most of my time with my mom until she passed away. When she passed away, interestingly enough, starting at age 14, I was independent and basically kept on living where I was living with her . . . under my grandmother's supervision.

In Paris I lived in an area called Republique, which is where all the cabinetmakers are. It was a semirough area, a nice area, a good place, but you learn fast. I was always very close to my dad, who was an engineer, and since I was like 12, 13 years old, I always worked in the summer at the cabinet shop doing cabinetmaking, just helping out. And with my dad, who was an aerospace engineer working on airplanes and stuff, I would actually help them out with drafting and stuff like that. So I learned on the spot a lot of engineering.

My dad was a very big influence on me, and I think his dad was a big influence on him, too, because they were all engineers and they passed on this tradition. He was involved in the most early times of numerical control machines; in fact, they had PDP-9s. They were the first people, I think, practically in the world to control machinery with PDP-9s.

His lifelong partner in business was Theo Williamson, who was also a big influence on me. He's the inventor of the hi-fi amplifier, the Williamson amplifier, and he became a member of the Royal Academy of Sciences.

Together, my dad and Theo built a lot of stuff and tried to build a lot of companies but never really made any money at it. Actually, they all got in financial trouble, but they always were making interesting things.

So I learned programming with these guys by just doing it on these PDP-9s and PDP-11s because they needed somebody else to do something and I was 13, 14, hanging around, so I said, "Okay, I'll do it."

I also learned something else from my dad, which was [that] he, by tradition, always played an instrument. He played the saxophone, so he taught me the saxophone, too, which kind of allowed me to start playing with bands in high school. I was playing at bar mitzvahs and weddings at 17 and 18, which was kind of fun.

Pascal's Logic

I went to the ETH Zurich, home for Wolfgang Pauli and Einstein. It's a technology school, like Cal Tech. That's where I got into systematic programming.

I really wanted to be something like a mathematician or a theoretical physicist. But it turns out that when you study that in Zurich, you have to take a programming class. There was this professor, Niklaus Wirth, teaching this new thing he developed called Pascal. There were 300 students signed up for the Fortran class and 10 in the Pascal class. I said, I'll sign up for that one.

Pascal was a formalization of the methodologies to program and talk to a computing machine. It got me into understanding where things were going, where the technology was going in terms of division for the man-machine interface from a programming standpoint.

I spent a few years there and we basically built the first Pascal compiler for big machines. I learned a lot, but then it turned out that it was time for me to leave Switzerland. My grandma was living in the south of France, and I felt that I had to have a little presence there.

So I finished my master's and my graduate studies in computer science mathematics at the University of Nice, in the south of France.

I also spent some time in Grenoble, and I got in touch with the guys who were looking for guys to program an operating system and the tools. As a student, I took the job. I had no idea what I was doing and it turned out to be the first personal computer.

Even though the personal computer industry had a year's lead in Europe, it didn't take off over there because the idea the guys

who built this had was to replace the larger machines with this little computational device.

Europe wasn't ready for that, and Europe is really a fragmented market from a language-barrier standpoint. If you take
Europe as a whole, it's as big of a market as the United States. But
the United States is a homogeneous market. You've got everybody
speaking basically the same language. With a few variations, you
get the same fast-food places everywhere, the same habit. If you
know how to do something in New York, you know how to do
something in California. Things are similar. The ads run fundamentally the same everywhere.

Visa Carded

I really wasn't into business at the time. My interest has always
been in what technology can do to make life better. I came here
because I thought that's where I could have the most impact.

I got to the U.S. on a tourist visa. The reason I came here is
because I was in the high-tech world and I felt that this is where it
was happening. I had pretty good credentials because I had been
involved with the first-ever PC. When I got here that's what I
wanted to do, so I applied to work for HP and Apple, but those
larger companies wouldn't hire me. They'd figure out, after two or
three days, that they liked what I could do but they figured that I
didn't have a work visa. Large companies don't like to hire people
without a green card.

So I decided that, because they wanted to hire me, I would
become a consultant and be contracted for my services; that way,
there was no visa stuff.

I called the company Market in Time because my customers
were engineering types who wanted to get their products to market
in time. I was based in San Jose, actually, on Stevens Creek Boule-
vard. I just had rented an apartment there and lived there and put
in a bunch of phone lines. But very rapidly I moved to Santa Cruz

because I spent a weekend there and I said, "Hey, this is really nice for what I do; I might as well live here by the ocean."

So I started this little consulting company called Market in Time, MIT, but MIT also meant Massachusetts Institute of Technology. It was kind of a purposeful thing because I figured my customers were R&D types. They were VPs of engineering, and when they get a letter from MIT, I knew they would open it.

I didn't know anything about marketing. And so this kept on going and I ended up hiring a couple of guys to help me, 'cause I had too much work. That was the summer of '82 when I started that. But around April '83, I got a letter from the real Massachusetts Institute of Technology—several lawyers who told me, "Hey, you can't use our name."

I consulted with a lawyer who advised, "Yeah, you're better off changing your name." And that's how the company that I started became Borland, which was a made-up name.

I started in a space above a garage in Scotts Valley. This little garage was fixing classic Mercedes and Jaguars—really cool, old cars—and on top there was this space for rent. I rented it and that became the office. Eventually we packed up to 25 people into basically two rooms.

I never got venture capital; I never looked for venture capital. I ended up buying a lot of firms that were venture capital–backed, but Borland never raised venture capital. I build things in a very scrappy way, very low key. We spend very little and we actually build a positive profit and loss.

My first customer was Adam Osborne of Osborne Computer Corporation. He had this new version of the Osborne that he wanted to ship for Christmas that year, and they were in a total disaster in terms of development. So I said, "Fine, I'll take it over." And I actually did do that, and it worked.

They actually shipped the software, but I never got paid because they filed bankruptcy—but the word about me got out.

There's a lot of stories about the early days of Borland, some of them true. It turns out that once we had a product to ship, Turbo

At sea: Philippe Kahn takes the wheel,
always the captain of his ship.

Pascal, we didn't have an advertising budget, and we certainly didn't have venture capital. In fact, I didn't have time for that, just like I didn't have time for a green card. I just called up the advertising guy for *Byte* magazine and said, "Hey, you know, we know we have this great thing and, you know, we're gonna advertise it in every magazine but yours, so give us some credit." After a lot of discussion, I think he was impressed with what he saw and he gave us 90 days' credit. When the ad ran we got thousands of sales, and not only did we pay the magazine but we became one of their best customers, and so he was happy and we were happy.

There's a funny anecdote that is also absolutely correct about the Comdex show in the fall of '83 when the first Borland product came out.

I went there and I knew we had a good product. I got to the show a day early and I cornered Shelly Adelson, who was the guy who started Comdex and now owns the Venetian Casino in Vegas. I cornered him and—the same trick as with *Byte*—I said, "Give me some credit, 90 days or so, so that I can have a room to hold a press conference to demo this thing." I don't know if you know Shelly, but he said, "Well, I'm not gonna do that. Why should I do that?" After 15 minutes he just gets fed up with me. I was pretty much a pain in the butt for him, so he really gets fed up. He said, "Why don't you have your press conference at McDonald's?" And I said, "You know what? That's not a bad idea." So I had my first press conference, in '83, at McDonald's on the strip, and 20 people showed up. The press conference was great because it cost just a pack of fries to everyone.

Jazz   Session

Jazz is great, because you take a song and you never play twice the same thing, and I think that helps a lot. That culture is really one where you have to invent the future if you don't want to be a victim of the future. You just invent it; it's much better.

That's sort of what Borland was, and it worked. It really worked. I think those were some of the best years in the PC industry because everybody was like, "Wow, what are they gonna do next?" And it worked, because that's what marketing is about.

All over the industry, everybody was doing their thing and nobody knew what would happen next. This hadn't been done before. Nobody had any idea. It was about wowing people. This was the time where there were no rules and even when there were rules we would break the rules. Everybody did; Borland always did. Jobs did, too.

I think there was probably five, six, seven years from the early '80s until '89 or so where there was a convergence of people with a lot of energy, a lot of creativity, new stuff happening, and everybody's background having an impact.

Well, I think industries mature, you know, industries have life cycles just like anything else, like us. And I think after a while, a few things happened. Microsoft started consolidating market share on the operating system and using their position in the operating system to build positions everywhere else. It became really hard to be in the tools business, for example.

The Dark Years

Borland was really the first company that got hammered by Microsoft. At the time, people said, "Oh, the Borland guys don't know what they're doing." Now they say, "Oh, okay, now I understand what happened."

The tough years were around 1992, 1993, when really I realized that Microsoft was all out to get Borland and there was no way to preserve Borland's core business in growth because basically Microsoft was willing to give it away with the operating system to gain that share of what Borland was selling. It's really hard to compete with what's free. How much better do you need to be—and we were always better—to be able to sell against that?

At first I really scratched my head, and said, how do we do this? You build a business and all this happens that way. Clearly because Borland was the first company assaulted that way, the press certainly didn't understand that. They said, "Aw, these guys don't know what they're doing. We need professional management, yada, yada, yada, yada." They didn't understand it was really an issue of business model and the structure of the industry that was changing. You could argue that different management would have done something else, but really it was a very different issue than the management or operational issues. It was a change in the dynamics of a whole industry. And by 1993, I think I fundamentally realized that.

In 1993 is when I finally woke up and said, "We have to change the playing field." That was when everybody was starting to talk about the Internet. I went to the board and told them, "What we have here is really not gonna matter. We need to change, to change our business, our business model. We cannot be a tools company. We need to be an Internet company. We need to bet on this new platform that's coming out and that needs to happen and we need to bet on things that are not PCs because Microsoft is dominating that. Game over." I mean, they had won the war.

So we had a big board meeting and they were arguing that the government will never let Microsoft do that and they'll get sued for antitrust and all that. My point was, "It won't matter, it won't help you. By the time anything happens, if it happens, it won't matter. We've gotta rethink this because the PC platform, as such, is now dominated by Microsoft."

My plan was to go for this new space, which was the Internet, and the decision at the board meeting is [that] they wouldn't do it. So I put it on the table and say, "Well, guys, if that's the case I don't think I should be the one continuing to run this company. You guys should fire me, because I don't want to keep on doing that." And they did fire me. I walked away from the company I had spent years growing into a $500 million corporation.

The first newspaper articles were kind of a shock to me, because I didn't understand how all that worked. Then I realized that what goes up goes down and that I should not have believed what was said when people said I was a genius. I needed to focus on the next thing.

I think that's a very entrepreneurial thing—always being able to focus on the next thing. It's something you learn from any competitive sport. It's like anything else, you know—sailing is like that. You do a race and the race lasts an hour and a half, it's full of drama, but the next race has nothing to do with the first race and you gotta be able to say, "Hey, it's over." Next race, and focus on the next opportunity. And it's hard, but you learn how to do that.

My concern was really for the people in the company as well as for the customers. I felt that there was some very core innovation that was happening in Borland that may not be able to continue if the industry kept on in the present direction.

What I thought was, there is a new world of new devices that's gonna be much smaller than PC stuff. And there's this thing called the Internet that's gonna be the network that we always wanted and Microsoft may not dominate all these things, and that's where I should personally focus my energy because I'm kind of a technology guy.

I thought, if the board at Borland didn't want to do it, I was gonna do it somewhere else. And that's what I did.

I went to Aspen for a month, stayed at a place called the Hotel Jerome, which is downtown Aspen, snowboarded, and designed the plan for this new company that became Starfish with Sonia Lee. Sonia is an immigrant, too, from Korea. She studied mathematics and engineering. While there, we got married, too, because we figured that that would be one-stop shopping.

Riding the Crest

I like surfing, I like sailing, and when I was a kid I did a lot of martial arts. Now I'm a little bit too fat for that, so I just need to get back in shape. But I do a lot of sailing and we have two Siberian huskies.

We got into this Iditarod stuff a few years ago, 1997, and we decided to cover the Iditarod on the Web, which nobody had done. We took digital cameras and there was this big expedition to Alaska, and we had pictures sent from stops and things. It was great; it was a lot of fun.

I still play music. I play about 30 minutes to an hour a day. Just for myself. It's just a way to let off steam, and that's an important part of my process of thinking about things.

I have a 25-year-old daughter who's getting into med school, and I have a 23-year-old who also wants to do that. I have a 10-year-old son and a 2-year-old daughter, so I have them both at the university and in diapers, so I see all the sides of things.

If they told me they wanted to be entrepreneurs, I'd say, just do it. I think, what's to risk, really? If you think about it, if you're a healthy person and if you've got a skill, what I tell my kids, is—and maybe I was kind of flippant when I said it—just do it.

My advice to my kids was always: Get a technology education that gives you an engineering skill or a skill that you can market, which is what my family's always done. Maybe a doctor, and that's about all that's acceptable. And maybe an artist if you're really talented—that's really hard.

I'm not sure they listen, but maybe you repeat it enough, they kind of do that. And once you have that, what's to risk? So you bet everything, what's gonna happen? You've got a skill; you can always get a job as an engineer. Even in the Borland days I'd say, "Hey, if this doesn't work out, big deal, you know? I started as an engineer, I'm still that."

I don't know what an entrepreneur is, but to me it's the difference between a jazz musician and a classical musician. I think a classical musician is a kind of guy who's gonna work for a big company. A jazz musician's gonna work in a small band and know how to improvise. I think that's really the analogy, that's really the difference.

Being an entrepreneur is liking the excitement of creating new things, something new that's never been done before. That's really what it's about. To me, it was never about making money; to me, that was always a by-product of being successful, but success started by doing something exciting.

The bottom line is if you're really innovating, if you're really creating new things, things that nobody's done before. There's nowhere to look to see how to do it, and sometimes even the business model is very new. You have to be ready to invent the future, because if you don't invent the future then you're gonna live in somebody else's future.

I haven't seen Philippe Kahn since the interview. Nor have I heard anything about his new companies. But I'm not concerned: Philippe will be back. He can't stay away. In the meantime, I went back and listened to one of his CDs. Like Kahn himself, it was better than I expected.

Photo by John Harding

John Sidgmore
Chairman and CEO, eCommerce Industries, Inc.
Vice Chairman, WorldCom

The Man
- Born on April 9, 1951
- Raised in Spring Valley, New York
- Earned a B.A. in economics at State University of New York
- Married, one child

The Entrepreneur
- Appointed CEO of UUNet in 1994; sold to MFS and then to WorldCom in 1996, where he took on the role of vice chairman
- Oversaw the acquisition of MCI, a company three times the size of WorldCom
- The combined company is a provider of global communications and managed network services with year 2000 revenues of $39.1 billion
- Cofounded eCommerce Industries, Inc., in 1999

"First of all, if you really believe strongly that you have to do something, do it hard, and work at it as hard as you possibly can. Worry about it every single day, because even the best businesses can go under. IBM proved that in the '80s; AT&T proved that in the early '90s. Nobody is immune. Life is moving so fast in the business world today, especially in technology. You're always worrying, moving, changing your strategy, and checking things out."

*I*t is a rule of thumb that all successful entrepreneurs have something about them that is extraordinary, almost superhuman. They seem to understand technology or markets or human behavior better than anybody else. Or they have a kind of supernatural will to succeed. Or they are functional sociopaths, capable of serially embracing, then abandoning, people according to the needs of the moment. Some seem to understand customers' desires even better than the customers themselves. And many, perhaps most, have a gift for convincing other talented people to join them on a crusade.

John Sidgmore, the man who runs the backbone of the Internet as director of UUNet, is certainly a man of considerable intelligence. He is also, by most accounts, an effective team builder and a pretty good technologist. But what makes him a great entrepreneur, the part of him that is superhuman, is his energy.

People who speak of that energy do so with a certain awe. I had heard the stories about Sidgmore's intensity and was looking forward to seeing it close up. Even more, I wanted to understand where it came from. Why would someone this successful, at the top of his game, still feel the need to live his life in a blur? Obviously, it wasn't for fame or power or money. There had to be something else in his past or in his makeup.

Not unexpectedly, interviewing Sidgmore was like wrestling a badger. Compact, impeccable, and intense, Sidgmore wasn't unfriendly, just focused. His words came out in machine-gun bursts, with the occasional hot tracer round to keep himself on target—and me on my toes.

Yet if John Sidgmore was pugnacious, he was also forthcoming. As he told me the story of his father's illness and its consequences for John's career, it dawned on me that his was a story not of ambition but of a man in a lifelong race against time. John Sidgmore lives his life the way he plays golf—indifferent to the score, but always with one eye on the clock.

Guitars and Golf

I enjoy all kinds of rock and roll. I like old stuff like [the] Rolling Stones. I like U2. I liked Nirvana until Kurt Cobain died. I'm really big into dead rock and rollers.

I started playing electric guitar when I was in college. I was never very good at it. But I liked it. I still play the same songs I played then, but I've added two songs a year. I have a bunch of amps and guitars, but the only person who will listen to me is my wife, and even she's tired of it. It's not like I'm opening at the Palladium or anything.

I also enjoy golf. It's funny because it is one of those sports that, 10 years ago, I thought you only play when you're 60 or 65 because it's kind of a slow-moving game. And that has become my only problem with the game—it takes about four or five hours to get through a round. So when I play, I try to go as fast as possible so that I can get done in two or three hours. I do it as late at night as possible or early in the morning when the courses aren't as crowded. The objective is to finish early. I don't care what the score is. I just want to be done.

Growing Up

I grew up in Spring Valley, New York, which is about 20 miles north of New York City. Just your basic suburbia.

We used to travel into the city every now and then to see a Yankees game or something. We would walk across the George Washington Bridge. You'd be crazy to try that today.

When I was 11 or 12 years old, we had two or three neighborhoods next to each other and I delivered newspapers to all of them. There were maybe 150 houses, which normally would have been three paper routes, but I somehow worked it so I got them all. I also mowed everybody's lawn and worked in my dad's office. So I was basically working full-time.

I'm naturally hyperactive. As a kid, I wasn't smashing my head against the wall or doing anything dangerous to other kids, but I was always very intense. Now, I drink 15 to 20 cups of coffee a day. I actually accentuate the hyperactivity by drinking more coffee.

I don't sleep a lot. I never really have. I wake up at eight o'clock in the morning and sleep maybe four or five hours a night. I've always felt like you live longer because you're up longer. If you stay up 20 hours a day, you actually have more time to live. Of course, my doctor says it's not actually like that. It's more like a car. The mileage counts, too.

Second Sight

I had a normal high school life. I played basketball, though I was never tremendously athletic. I'm not that tall or fast, so sports weren't really the center of my life in high school. But I had a great time. I did reasonably well in school and I felt pretty good about myself when I graduated.

My dad was probably the most important person in my life. My mom was a housewife, and she worked in the office with him. They were kind of a working unit. Dad's office was maybe a mile away, which was a long way away in my little town.

My father always taught me that if I work hard, always keep going, and never give up, I could accomplish anything. And those things stuck with me.

When I was about to graduate high school, my dad had a series of operations for his eyesight. His work was in jeopardy because he was an accountant, and, more importantly, a sole proprietor. So I stayed home to help him run his business. This meant that I had to go to school somewhere near home. We had a close-knit family, and I knew that this was just something I had to do and there was no question about it.

We weren't wealthy by any means, but we certainly weren't poor. We had everything we wanted when we were kids and when my dad went through that period, it was a tough time, but it wasn't really a disaster financially. He was insured, so that wasn't really the question. The question was how to keep the business going while he was gone.

I had been working in the office with him pretty regularly for four or five years, part-time. And, of course, my mom had to take him in to the hospital every day to get eye treatments and so forth, so that was sort of the beginning of my professional career.

The Dismal Science

I went to community college right around the corner for the first two years, to be close to home. Then I went off to Oneonta, which was only two and a half hours away, so I could come back and forth if I had to. Only New York state people would know that school, but it's a teachers' college on the top of a mountain.

It turned out to be a great experience, and I got a lot of good feelings about myself from knowing I was helping out my father. I also knew clearly then that I was not going to be an accountant. For one thing, I couldn't write in those little ledger books—my handwriting is pretty bad.

I really floundered around in terms of what I wanted my career to be and what I wanted my major to be. It had changed three or four times. At first it was chemistry, then history, which I really loved. It took me some time to discover what I wanted to do.

My dad told me right before I graduated that there wasn't a big calling for historians anymore, and that I'd probably wind up as a teacher. I knew I definitely didn't want to be a teacher. So I quickly changed my focus to economics and took all of the required classes in my last year and graduated in economics.

I never expected to be an economist. I'm not sure I even knew what an economist was in my earlier years. My cousin, whom I was pretty close with at one time, was a computer salesperson. This was back in the early '70s when computers were these mystical things, very interesting and exciting. What I liked about this industry was that it was a brand new industry with all young people. You didn't have to sit through 47 chairs in order to get to a senior position, like in most large corporations where you start out sitting at a gray metal desk and then you graduate little by little. I liked it because if you went in and you were successful, you could move up quickly. I was extremely impatient.

I first worked for a little company called Unicom. We sold electronic calculators, what we called minicomputers. Those things were pretty large back then. They weighed around 35 pounds, and in order to be in this business you had to be pretty strong so you could carry them around to show people.

I'm actually not a naturally talented salesman in the traditional sense. I was never any good at schmoozing. But I always figured out a way to win. I worked harder than anybody else and found a way to get in. I did research on the accounts and always felt like I could win if I could just work harder than anybody else—which I did.

I was with Unicom for four months, and then another company developed this thing called the Bowmar Brain, which was the first real tiny electronic calculator.

The calculators that I was selling cost $2,500. When I saw this Bowmar Brain that weighed a couple ounces and only cost a hundred bucks, I said, "You know, I don't think I'm gonna win against this. I think this company's gonna die." So I left.

Then I went to a company called Computer Design, which really had state-of-the-art products. They were like Hewlett-Packard programmable calculators, years before they were famous. They had geometric functions and trigonometric functions, and I would take these in to laboratories, like Bell Labs and Union Carbide Labs, and the scientists would grab them right out of the box and want to buy them. I came home and told my wife, "This is the easiest job in the world. These things cost five, six, seven thousand dollars, and they sell themselves."

Well, the company was run by a genius. But he was also a bit crazy and had no experience in business. We were selling these things for about one-fourth what they really cost to make, so there was a reason why they were very attractive.

The company went bankrupt, and I wound up with a company called GE Information that sold computer time-sharing. Computer time-sharing was the up-and-coming framework. It was a large-scale network around the world that they had built, and they were selling the use of that network in combination with applications. So if you could learn something about somebody's business, you could figure out a way to help their business and write an application, then sell it over your network.

It really was the forerunner of the Internet. When I joined the company, they paid me what seemed like an outrageous amount of money. I think they paid me $10,000 a year and fairly high commission. It was a fantastic job.

I was there for about 14 years, during which I worked my way up to the position of general manager of North America. I had about a thousand people working for me. That was one good thing about the company. I moved up pretty quickly, and I was one of the youngest section managers they had.

Being in Charge

I had a couple of different mentors. One in particular, named Tom Vincey, helped me when I was a young manager. But I started to get increasingly frustrated because the company was stagnant to a certain extent. We needed a lot more investment. We needed to take many more risks, and GE didn't really want us to take more risks at that time. I knew that if I could have gotten them to make some investments, I could have made the company greater.

The computer and information business was really GE's Achilles' heel. They never really got it. So I left to take over a very small company called CSE. It was a privately owned, dying company. The owner wanted somebody to come in and turn it around, energize it, and then sell it.

I always liked being in charge. I liked to go out, make the mistakes, do it my way, and make it work or die trying. That's what I wanted at the time and I didn't really care what the title was.

I was 37 years old and my parents thought I was absolutely nuts for leaving GE. My wife was tremendously supportive. She's been my partner all along, and that's partly because she really understood. She had her own software company in the early '80s, so she knew what I was going through.

I joined CSE and turned it around. When I got there, we had no international operations. About half our revenue was international when I left. We had big, growing operations around the world. We built it into a $100 million company and then sold it three years later to Computer Sciences. I actually stayed at CSE for a couple of years as the CEO just to make sure it worked well into the new culture.

I felt a responsibility to the people. I wanted to make sure that it worked well. And I felt a responsibility to the company I sold it

Small deal: John Sidgmore, growing up very fast.

to. I felt loyal. We'd told them it was a good company and I wanted to make sure it integrated well. And it did.

Different people have different phases of a company's growth that they like. Some people like three people sitting in a garage on cardboard boxes, and some people like newly public companies, and some people like standing like [a] colossus over a giant corporation.

Standing like [a] colossus probably isn't my number one thing. I think that the real kick is taking something small—whether you start it from scratch or have 50 or 75 people—and turning it into a bigger company that's on a real positive track. To me that's the kick. That's where you get the energy from.

Oui-Oui

I got a call from the venture capitalist who originally put money into UUNet. He was a guy that I worked with years before at GE and now wanted me to come on board UUNet. I told him, "UUNet? That's ridiculous. It's a little, teeny company. I'm already running a hundred-million-dollar business." I soon found out that, though the company was small, it had great technology.

It was one of the first companies involved in Internet access. The more I read about it, the more I thought that this was a highly marketable technology. The company had no marketing at the time. I had a solid background in the network business with GE, so I started to see that this technology allowed for an interactive public network. I thought a business, for the first time in history, could go off and talk to *all* its customers, talk to *all* its employees and all its vendors on a single network that everybody would be connected to. That's really a powerful concept, especially five years ago. So we took a shot at it.

UUNet had been founded by a brilliant technologist named Rick Adams. He decided that he didn't want to have a little company. As good as it was technically, he wanted to build it into a big company. So he hired a venture capitalist to lend him some money and bring in a management team, which was remarkable foresight on his part at that time.

I went and interviewed with Rick, and I spent hours and hours with him. I met the technical people, and they were the traditional beard-and-sandals, brilliant engineer kind of guys. And I just fell in love with the place. It was very exciting and stimulating. I would tell people, "This thing could blow up completely in a couple months and never work, and I'll be back doing something else again. Or it could be spectacularly successful. But either way it's going to be a hell of a lot of fun."

A lot of times those things don't work out. It often happens that the founder, the technical guy, resents the business guy who comes in as CEO and takes over his company. Rick was tremendous from day one. We got along famously. We traveled together everywhere, and he was like having a CD-ROM of the Internet. You'd ask him a question and the perfect answer came back. So it was an easy environment for me to plug into.

I took over UUNet in early '94, and it's been a spectacular rocket ride. First of all, you have to remember, this was really before most people had ever heard of the Internet. Today, everybody thinks they're an expert. But nobody really knew what it was back then. It was this mystical thing. It was controlled by heavyweight technical guys who spoke their own language and had their own special decoder rings. If you didn't have one, you couldn't talk to them.

When I came in, the company had been built up to about $4 or $5 million in revenues. We had 40 employees, almost all technical, I mean super-heavyweight technical guys. And we only had one sales guy.

And the company's name, let's face it, was UUNet. It meant UNIX-to-UNIX Network. When I took it over, I told my wife, "The first thing I'm going to do when I get in there is change that ridiculous name." It sounds like wee-wee net or yo-yo net, and it doesn't sound professional.

But the name grew on me. We went public. Bill Gates announced our partnership. I was starting to like this UUNet thing, and I said, "Well, when you have two U's, you have to make it unique." So we had all kinds of campaigns about that.

Ramp-up

My strategy was that we were going to avoid the consumer market. Everybody was talking about AOL and selling to consumers online at night and changing the social structure and all that. I said, "Well, we're gonna focus on the business market, where companies are used to spending thousands of dollars a month on networks." This was less expensive, more powerful, and that was really kind of what differentiated UUNet at the end of the day.

Then I said, "You know, we want to build this huge network so we get scale economics, and the only way to do that is to build the network out for the business marketplace." Businesses use it during the day. "And then we'll sell it for a cheap price at night to the consumer providers on a wholesale basis." We went to AOL and went to Microsoft and said, "Hey, we're gonna have this huge network. We'll let you use it at night. We'll share the economics, and it'll be great for everybody." And that's what happened.

We put together a plan at the end of '94 that said that we would get to $100 million in two years. We did it in a year. And then we said we'd get to $300 million. The next year we got to $500 million. So we were always way ahead of our plans. But when we knew it was really going to work was when we closed the Microsoft contract. That gave us daytime and nighttime usage. We were the only company on the Internet at the time that was profitable. I would argue [that] today we may still be the only company that's ever been profitable on the Internet.

I don't think we thought about being kings of the Internet. It was just a very exciting time for a little, dinky company like UUNet. Bill Gates got up on the stage and announced this partnership with UUNet. It was pretty remarkable.

In retrospect, we really were the best network on the Internet at that time. Because we were the underlying network for AOL, or at least most of its business, we had a very significant percentage of the consumers that were on the network. The Europeans did some traffic assessments, and they concluded our traffic percentage was about 30 to 50 percent of all the traffic on the Internet.

Looking back, it's amazing how tiny UUNet was four or five years ago. There were all these big telephone companies that were competing against us at the time—and now UUNet is much larger than them. And that was largely a function of early relationships with Microsoft and AOL.

I sold UUNet to a company called MFS in early '96 because we wanted access to their telecommunications facilities. I became president of MFS, and then four months later I sold the whole thing to WorldCom and became vice chairman of WorldCom. Our strategy at the time was to continue to treat this as a development project, because deregulation and the Internet had really changed the industry. We thought that if we kept moving, we could change the landscape. So we went out and acquired as aggressively as we could, and deployed capital.

Through that whole thing we wound up buying MCI, which nobody in the world believed was possible. It was a company three times our size, and we found a way to pull it off. And we never really anticipated the strength with which the government would come at us for UUNet, because here we had this big MCI piece and WorldCom and all these huge players, and suddenly the world was frightened to death of little old UUNet. It wasn't so little then. But to me it was always this terrific little company, and suddenly it had become very large.

There was some question by regulators about whether selling off MCI's Internet assets would be acceptable. They really wanted us to sell off UUNet before they would approve the merger. We made it clear up front we would not have merged with MCI if we had to sell UUNet, as ridiculous as that sounded. We thought UUNet was really the rocket, and we were right.

Bernie Evers and I would look at this merger and say, "We're going to have 70,000 employees." Bernie had a start-up 10 years ago and he bought a whole bunch of little companies and all of a sudden became bigger and bigger and did an unbelievably fantastic job. We did the same thing and never thought of ourselves as a big company. Now we have 65-, 75,000 people. We had the UUNet all-employee meeting out in Virginia a few weeks ago, and we had to use the whole warehouse. We used to hold it in the conference room.

The merger itself was a $38 billion merger. It was the largest in history at the time we did it. Nobody really looked at it that way because nobody believed it was even possible for us to buy MCI, but the numbers were actually spectacular. The financial support for this deal was fantastic and the synergies between the two companies were terrific. So we never really looked back.

Racing the Clock

People always ask, "What are you worried about?" I always say, "Everything." I mean, our industry's changing so fast. There are so many new players. There are so many challenges. We worry about everything all the time.

Microsoft may be one of the few companies that is worse at talking to Washington politicians than we were. Growing up as a small company, we never really learned how to do that and never focused on doing that. We probably didn't do enough of it. But, by the time it was over, I had spent an awful lot of time with the Department of Justice and the SEC and the European Union and I knew more lawyers than you ever wanted to know in your life, believe me.

It was a difficult time because there's a lot of politics surrounding this, and a lot of it is a PR war. So you have to fight what seem to be fake battles. It's different than real business, where you're trying to sell customers and build technology. That's why I think running a large company, especially in a partially regulated industry like communications, is very much different than a start-up.

I think all of us within the MCI WorldCom senior management team who started off in an entrepreneurial environment or a start-up look back at those days fondly.

I think I've been able to move and change in my life. I've made a number of changes in job types and careers. I've had big jobs, moved to small jobs, and then back to big ones. So I feel like I'll be able to make the changes required. And when it's no longer fun, I'll stop doing it and do something else.

I think my father and mother always thought I would be successful, but they never pushed me to be successful in any specific way. They just wanted me to be the best at what I did.

It's funny: When I went to UUNet, I was the second-oldest one there. I think I was 39 or 40, and the guy who was the oldest was 46. They called him Pops. The guy's 46 years old. The average age then was 22 or something. I think the average age is 25 now.

But you really do need a balance. The passion and the energy of the young entrepreneurs is fantastic. And you need one or two slightly older guys that remember how things did or didn't work.

There's no equation to making business work that you can plug in. Every situation's different. Every era's different. Every industry is different. You have to move and change with the times. On the other hand, you have to remember historical events so that at least you can watch out for certain things. That's why you need a balance.

〰️

I was a little taken aback, but not completely surprised, when John Sidgmore told me during the interview how many cups of coffee (15 to 20) he drank each day. That seemed superhuman—and a little unbelievable. Like many entrepreneurs, was he merely exaggerating to enhance his myth? But as he headed out the door, Sidgmore was overheard to mutter to a staffer, "I need to get a cup of coffee before I drive to the airport. Is there any place nearby where I can stop?" The airport was only two miles away.

Photo by John Harding

Steve Wozniak
Cofounder, Apple Computer, Inc., Teacher

The Man
- Born August 11, 1950
- Raised in Sunnyvale, California
- Finished his college education at the University of California at Berkeley in 1986
- Remarried, six children

The Entrepreneur
- Invented the personal computer and cofounded Apple Computer, Inc., in 1976
- Apple year 2000 revenues: $8 billion (fiscal year ending 9/30/00)

"When a kid asks for advice, I always say if you're going to do something, make sure it's very high quality. Do it better than you could have done; after you're done, go back and do it again. When it's as good as you can do it, go back and do it again and make it a little better yet— something better that no other human being would have done. And make sure you always enjoy what you're doing."

$\mathcal{I}$ had two great reservations about having Apple cofounder Steve Wozniak (Woz) on the series. One was intellectual, the other personal.

Intellectually, I wasn't sure if Woz even qualified as an entrepreneur. Certainly he was one of the great inventors of the age, and the Apple I and II among the greatest modern inventions. But Woz also had resisted the lure of entrepreneurship throughout most of the Apple era. It was his partner Steve Jobs who had cajoled, threatened, seduced, and manipulated Woz into designing products and even joining the young company. Left to his own devices, Woz would likely be receiving his 25-year pin as a product engineer at Hewlett-Packard right about now.

On the personal side, I had just published a major 600-page book on the story of Apple Computer and, though Wozniak was unquestionably among the more appealing characters, it was definitely a book without heroes.

I had known about Woz for many years. While I was going to school with Jobs in Mountain View, Woz was on the swim team with buddies of mine. When I moved to Sunnyvale, he was a neighbor. I watched the two Steves, along with the son of my Sunday school teacher, buy parts for the Apple I. And I was in the Wozniak living room watching when Mr. Jerry Wozniak, Steve's father, complained to marketing guru Regis McKenna about the bad influence an odd young man—Steve Jobs—was having on his son.

I was also at the Wescon trade show to see the first public unveiling of the Apple computer. One of my first stories as a cub reporter was a profile of the newly successful Apple Computer, Inc., where I officially met Woz for the first time. And I was there at the Macintosh introduction, which effectively marked the end of the Wozniak era at Apple.

Since then, we had crossed paths on a number of occasions. And in the years in between, I occasionally talked to his mother and was brought up to date.

But it was while writing *Infinite Loop*, the book about Apple, that I found myself living—at least mentally—on a daily basis with Steve Wozniak for much of two years. In the pages of the book, I recounted Woz's story, from the early outburst of genius to the troubled years as a phone hacker, the years of fame and frustration under the control of Jobs. It was not a happy story. Arguably, Woz had been set up and ripped off by Jobs, his best friend. Yet Jobs had also coerced Woz into producing the invention that would make Woz's name all but immortal. And then the long postscript: the plane crash, the failed rock festivals, the long alienation from Apple Computer. If in the end I portrayed Woz as happy, it might seem to many readers as small consolation.

Yet the more I thought about Steve Wozniak, the more it seemed to me that he was a rare example of someone who had lived an entrepreneurial career backwards. He had, remarkably, invented a legendary product, worked in a landmark start-up company, and become a tycoon . . . and only then did he begin to take command of his life and construct a career of his own devising. Since then, he has been a rock impresario, a company founder and CEO, and a noted philanthropist. Steve Wozniak is more an entrepreneur now than when he was celebrated for being one.

Nevertheless, even if I could accept the idea of Woz as a subject for the series, I still wasn't anxious to see him. There was a lot of history between us, and I assumed he'd read the nastier bits in the book. So when he arrived on the set, I wasn't sure what attitude he'd take. Sure, he'd accepted the appearance, but that could have been merely for the opportunity to tell me off.

I should have known better. After all, one of the truest things I'd ever written about Woz was that he was the Candide of Silicon Valley. No matter what had happened in the past, Woz was, as always, cheerful, enthusiastic, and nobody's fool. The resulting conversation was a rare glimpse into what it is like to be in the grip of a kind of divine madness, a genius that enables you to not only build a machine, but actually think like it—and how that brief moment can change your life forever.

I was the luckiest person in the world to grow up in a nice, new community [Sunnyvale, California], when there weren't traffic problems, you could park anywhere you wanted to. Down the street there was an orchard. And I'd walk the other way, and there was an orchard. You had to ride your bike through orchards to get to school, but I loved it. I loved it. I really want to get out of the Silicon Valley now. I want to get back to that.

I had so many friends in the neighborhood, and we all did the same things—we rode our bikes, we built house-to-house intercoms. There were a lot of kids that were interested in electronics, and parts, and how to make them work. What happens is, if you mention something interesting about electronics that interests you, and another kid is interested in the same thing, it motivates you, because, hey, you're both interested in it. This must be a good way to go. And there were a lot of fathers who were engineers in the neighborhood, too.

My dad worked at Lockheed. When I look back, my father was a critical factor in inculcating engineering. He didn't push it, but when I asked a question or wanted help in that direction, he would go to a blackboard and write something new, one step deeper—a circuit, an equation. In fifth grade, I even had a ham radio license. You have to learn a bit of electronic circuitry—and I did that on my own. I mean, he almost didn't know I was doing it.

My mom was the nicest mom. She was always joking with us, and laughing and friendly. And you know, the type of person I am more comes from my mom. My father was a little bit more strict and tense because of the tough engineering life at Lockheed.

Touched by Fire

I got really interested in electronics around junior high school. I owe it to science fairs. For science fairs you had to think of a project. Usually, my dad would suggest a project. I learned a little electronics with the first one, and the next one I learned more.

I would get kits for Christmas and just start building them. And in about the fifth grade, we made a very complicated circuit with a hundred switches to switch on different sets of lights that corresponded to electrons and the atom. That was a major project for a fifth-grader. By sixth grade, it all happened. It just all happened. In sixth grade, I studied this book about a language called Logic. I was a little bit mathematically advanced so I was able to understand logic and Boolean algebra and some equations for changing logic around. It was exactly the right start toward the next step toward learning all about computers.

I went to Homestead High School and took one of the very few electronics classes at a high school in America during that era.

I can't imagine another electronics class having ever been run so well. That teacher did an incredible job—he was an incredible man. For somebody like me that was so advanced in electronics, he got me into a company to learn how to program computers. He found me something outside of school. He didn't say, "Inside of school is all we provide you." He actually went beyond that for any students that needed it.

In high school, my peer group was people interested in electronics, but none of them were like me. None of them were brilliant and taught math students and received 800s on college entrance exams. So I was kind of rare, and even though I had a clique around me, I was always the leader, because I was the most intelligent, and they were generally younger than me.

Even though I didn't have the normal social structure, I was in clubs and in athletics at school. Since I wasn't "in," I developed the idea by the end of high school that, "I don't care what they think—I'll be myself, and I'm not going to be subject to peer pressure." I read books like *Walden* and I just got very strong feelings that I wasn't going to follow others. There was this idea of being an individual and not conforming. I saw everybody around me conforming, going to parties and doing the same things, and I said, "I'm not going to do that." I will decide for myself—that's how I was.

Homebrew

I was really advancing myself in electronics and design and working at Hewlett-Packard as an engineer even though I didn't have a college degree, and I was designing a ton of electronics projects on the outside. I had a lot of friends that would call and say, "Hey, Steve, can you design a little circuit that could help us put movies into this hotel?" This was way back before it happened. And I'd get a little job, and I'd get to design a circuit and run down to Los Angeles and help them set it up and show it off. And another guy would want a pinball game, and I'd design it. And Atari wanted a Pong-ish game, and I designed that for them. I was just constantly doing electronics on the side for fun; not for a salary, not for any clothes to wear, not for any title or big name or anything.

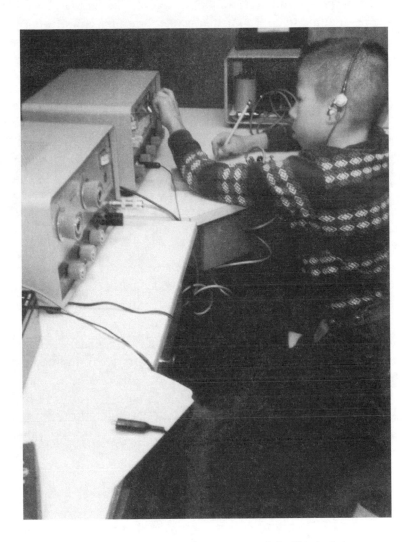

Tuned in: Little Stevie, the Mozart of the Digital Age, at play.

Then this club started and I kind of got tricked into it. I would have been afraid to go if I knew it was a computer club. I went to the Homebrew Club meeting and it was so amazing. I just sat there, spellbound by this whole thing that was happening. The picture of the first hobbyist computer—it looked like a big, ugly, commercial mainframe computer, but it was a computer, and that's what my whole life was about. I had built one of those myself, five years before—a little, tiny computer called the Cream Soda Computer that burned up the day the newspapers came out to take a picture of it.

So I went to the Homebrew Club, and I found out all these people were into this new thing about microprocessors—computers. They were all technicians that loved computers. They would find surplus parts and build their own world.

They were just people that were interested in computers because they could have a computer and they knew how to connect it to some railroads and run their little rail trains around. I was like them in that sense, but their ability to design wasn't there.

The first night, at that very first meeting, I saw that I was going to actually have a commercial product computer in my life, and that dream had become real. I saw this unbelievable thing that a whole bunch of people like myself wanted computers. And I had told my dad, "Someday, I'm going to own a computer even if I can't afford a house. I'll live cheaply—I'm going to get a computer someday in my life."

Digital Dreams

I was dreaming in assembly language. I would go to sleep with a problem in my head and I'd wake up in the middle of the night with a solution and write it down.

The Apple I had basically no operating system. The Apple II had a little mini-operating system. The Apple I just had a little, tiny program built in; you could start typing in base-16 numbers. I'd

type 'em and type 'em and type 'em and I would write down programs in this hexadecimal arithmetic. That was the only way I
could do it. I could not afford any devices that would do it automatically. I did that every day. I was working on [it] and [I would]
add a few things and test it out and debug it and keep running it
and get more and more things working. It was unbelievable. I look
back and I think, "How could anyone ever have done that?" But it
was the only way I had.

I would just walk around with the programs I was writing for
the early Apples in my head, and I would just constantly think of
this one little section of code, maybe about 20 steps, or is there a
technique that can squeeze in an idea? And every once in a while,
in the middle of the day, an idea pops in; you set it down on paper,
and you find out, "Oh, I just squeezed 20 bytes down to 18!"

You can write a program—a very good program—and you can
work to make it even better, and it's great. Or you can work on it, and
work on it and work on it until every ounce of everything you could
ever come up with is in it. That's art. And that's exactly what I did.

All of the Apple I and Apple II years, those early years of Apple,
any project I worked on had to have such extreme attention that no
other person would have gone that far; they all would have given
up earlier because it was done and it was working. And who's going
to see if it's art? But a true artist would do it for its own sake.

The disk drive that I developed at Apple was a real good example of that. I didn't really know how to design one, but when I was
done, it was only five chips, and it worked. And I opened up a competitor's schematic to figure out, "What did I leave out?" They have
50 chips. And I looked at their schematic, found out that mine did
more, and it did it a lot simpler and more directly.

I also wrote the programs for Apple, and the code; and I
designed it, built it, and soldered it together. Then I sat with an
oscilloscope and looked at all the signal traces, and analyzed what
was wrong and improved it and fixed it and debugged it. I even sat
with tape and laid out the PC board. Crossing all of those disciplines is something that it was a rare point in time where one per-

son could build a full, complete product covering a lot of the disciplines to get the whole thing done.

There was a short, short little window of time for just a few years where one person could build a whole computer—something that was extremely valuable. Before us, it took teams of engineers to handle the huge, room-size computers, just for the housing alone. It would take huge teams to build huge computers. Now, a computer is so valuable, there's so many billions of dollars associated with computer platforms, that there's always a huge team of engineers put on it to do the best job possible.

I wasn't trying to make something that was somehow better sellable. My rewards were inside. Nobody would ever see them; I had goals of my own. I wanted to know that I could do the most perfect job. I wanted to make the machine that I could use in my own life. I had the artistic freedom, too. If I hadn't had that kind of freedom, and if I hadn't been able to cover all these little disciplines, I don't know if I would have been as motivated. If I couldn't see the final product of what I wanted and knew how valuable it could be, I don't know if I would have been motivated enough to work like that.

Apple Computer

I loved HP, and I had found the love of my life being an engineer. I wanted to be an engineer my whole life, and I found the place I could do it. I had engineers around me that were friends. We'd go flying in their airplanes. We had such a fun time in that lab; doing our work was fun.

I was so loyal to HP; I offered the Apple I and the Apple II to HP first. I wanted them to do it. I believed in them, and I really wanted them to do this computer.

I designed the Apple I, but I couldn't get HP to build it. I really wanted them to. So Steve [Jobs] said, "Well, why don't we build it?" And I said, "First, well, look, I owe it to HP first." So I offered them the Apple I, and they didn't want to do it.

I now realize they couldn't have done it, because they would have done it the HP way. When they finally built their own computer, they did it the HP way, which was wrong for the starting machine that would really reach people.

Steve said, "Okay, well, we'll pay this guy a few hundred bucks to lay out a PC board, and we'll kind of get it made over in Santa Clara for this much, and we'll need a few hundred bucks each." And I sold my calculator, you know. Big risk. I mean, this was the most valuable thing that I owned, my HP-65 calculator. I loved it. I had to sell it for $500, but then again, we were coming out with the HP-67, and my employee price would be $370. So it's like I didn't even take a financial risk. I didn't leave my job.

I designed the Apple I and the Apple II and the cassette interfaces and the floppy interfaces and whatever else came along. I wrote tons of software and demos and operating systems and the BASIC language—I wrote it all on my own time at my cubicle at Hewlett-Packard and my apartment.

I was designing hardware and writing software that I was proud of. It was my life, so I had my reward. I didn't need to start a company. I really had to be talked into it. I told Steve I didn't think we'd get our money back. He said, "Well, we'll have a company for once." And it was just a little, tiny deal; and then he got a $50,000 order and that was a little bit of a shock.

I came up with this incredible, incredible invention of the Apple II. It's just too hard to say how many new things it had. It had color, and it had graphics, and it had sound—it was the most amazing device, ever. We started thinking, this could be the device that can really make a million dollars. We started looking around for companies to buy it for a lot of money. I was shocked that he seemed to be talking, like, hundreds of thousands of dollars. How can you sell a half a year of my work for hundreds of thousands of dollars? I couldn't understand that concept, but he was trying to.

Ultimately, Steve brought in venture capitalists who would talk to us and say, "How many? What do you think the market is for these?" I said, "A million computers." He said, "Why do you say a million?" I said, "Well, because there's a million ham radio opera-tors, and computers is bigger than ham radio." Which is so true, but it's not business.

He eventually got us onto Mike Markkula—and Steve went over and met [with] Mike for quite a while. Steve convinced Mike of the market and the potential for computers in people's lives and chang-ing the world, and Mike believed in computers in the home all his life. They hit it off very well, and it came to a point that Mike said there was one little thing: I would have to leave Hewlett-Packard. And I thought, "I've done all this incredible designing for over a year now, and I've done it and had my job at Hewlett-Packard—I've been able to moonlight. Why don't I keep the job at Hewlett-Packard for my lifetime security with the company I love, and we'll start Apple anyway?" And he said, "Nope. Got to leave Hewlett-Packard."

I thought it over and thought it over in my head. I knew that I wanted to write programs on computers, and that had nothing to do with the company. I was going to be happy in my life if I had a job for life at Hewlett-Packard, and I could do these fun things that I loved. So I said, "No. Not going to do Apple." Mike just sort of said, "Okay, that's fine." Steve was kind of upset.

Steve got all my relatives and friends to call me up and, finally, one of them talked me into it. I could go and start Apple and just be an engineer my whole life, and that was okay, and just use Apple as a way to make money off my design.

As soon as somebody said I could be an engineer my whole life, I felt better. I felt if I went in trying to run the business and making design decisions, and didn't have the artistic freedom, I'd eventually be squeezed out and have nothing to show for it and no job at Hewlett-Packard.

By the time I left Apple, we had 50 engineers to do any job. I had good jobs and I was doing good work, but I wasn't critical to the success of the company anymore. At that point in time, I had my plane crash, and so I got to leave the company gracefully.

There was an article the other day in the newspaper and it said, "Well, survivors of plane crashes generally have better mental health." And I always feel, "Why do I always feel happy? Why am I always of a good opinion about life?" The plane crash gave me a little time to take off because I wasn't really needed at Apple, and didn't want to just be there as a symbol. After the plane crash, when I finally woke up from amnesia about five weeks later, I said, "This is the last chance of my life to get a college degree." My father gave me real strong values about education and college, and how that's how you get somewhere in life. And I wanted to show that for my kids, and I had three good years of college done. I didn't drop out; I didn't say, "College is lousy." I didn't say, "College is hard." I just took a year off to earn money for my fourth year of college, and it took a while to earn it. [*Laughs.*] So that plane crash has been a blessing in so many ways. I was going to finish college. And I did.

For the Kids

Even as a child, you're taught some things are good and some are bad and some people are willing to give what they have to be helpful. These are all good values to children. Now, we grow up and we get a little bit more adult-like and have to think about, "Nah, I want to invest it and have it maximize in this percentage per year." But I didn't really grow up; I always had an idea that I was going to stay younger longer, like some people do. I thought back to, "What are the true values?" You know, "What's really good?"

I would listen to people talk about something they had planned—the Children's Discovery Museum was probably the real first big one that I got involved with. These were good people that had good ideas, that wanted to do good things related to children and the community. I just couldn't see a group working that hard, that many people, and having so many good ideas, and so many project ideas and concepts of what the thing would be, and not having the money—people willing to give them money for it.

It was nice to be recognized for helping the museum. People

ask me all the time, what am I most proud of, and I say, "I have a street named after me!"

I thought one day, "What's important to me?" And I came up with schools, children that were learning, and computers. And the two of those go together, so I started to get involved with my own district. At first, it was easy to just provide computers because every school back then wanted to get a few computers and set up a lab. Then, I started feeling like, "Well, when you give money, you're not really giving yourself, your time." So, I started teaching. I was scared. I didn't really know how to teach, and I had never studied teaching, but I was gonna do my best. I started with a couple of kids; and then 6 kids; and then two classes of 6 at once; and eventually, 22. Eventually, I said, "Okay, every year, the entire fifth grade of the school." I'm teaching kids about the age I was when I got interested in electronics.

Technology is changing so fast, and, as I get older, I don't change as well with it. I still read a newspaper in the morning, whereas all the young kids that are really into the computers are doing it all online.

I'm near it, I understand it, I see what's happening, and I see where it's at, and I can even talk about it and teach it. But my life can't be changed as much as the kids that are growing up with it. And it's still changing so much.

I'm not going to do the technology and the engineering for a company again, because the way I did it as an artist was giving the smallest little detail 24-hours-a-day attention. And you just can't live that way.

There's a few years in your life when you're young enough that you can do that, but you can't be that kind of designer forever, and I wouldn't want to just go out and be a little hack designer.

Perfect   Fun

I don't think of myself as "I changed the world," and somehow this period was the period that caused me to change the world. It just caused me to have some really great skills in an area that was going to change the world. I was just a really talented person at the right place, at the right time. Maybe I had some neat influences on just the right sort of combination of ideas and products that worked a certain way. And maybe I have reasons for why I did that, but if I hadn't, someone would have done it.

I just want to be known as a good engineer, but also one that wanted to make a computer fun. *[Laughs.]* To be known as having started a company is not something I ever would have wanted in my life. To be known for being a good engineer, doing some real clever things, or being a good father, or a real funny guy—those are the only things that mean something to me. I just sort of wound up in this incredible thing that was happening, and I had the great invention of the day.

In sixth grade, I told my dad, "I want to be an engineer first, like you; and I want to be a teacher, second. And I want to tell jokes," 'cause my mom always said, "Have a sense of humor." And you know what, to this day, the only thing I didn't ever count on was that I would be appearing before cameras, and I was way too shy, and that one I can't explain. But, other than that, my life went almost exactly as I would have wanted it to go. Just too lucky.

There was an interesting moment in the course of the interview that told me Steve Wozniak might not be as forgiving as he seemed. I had just made a statement about an event in the early days of Apple as part of a question. Woz began his reply by correcting me. Then, not even making a little smile of triumph, he looked me right in the eye and said evenly, "See? You didn't get everything right in your book." Then he instantly returned to the old, sunny Woz of legend. We didn't speak of our disagreements again that day. And we haven't since.

Photo by John Harding

Bob Metcalfe
Founder, 3Com

The Man
- Born on April 7, 1946 in Brooklyn, New York
- Earned a B.S. in electrical engineering and business management at MIT, and a master's degree in applied mathematics and a Ph.D. in computer science at Harvard University
- Married, two children

The Entrepreneur
- Invented Ethernet technology in 1973 and devised Metcalfe's law in 1980
- Cofounded 3Com in 1979
- 3Com is now a leading provider of networking products, with year 2000 revenues of $2.8 billion (fiscal year ending 5/31/01)
- Currently is a venture capitalist for Polaris Ventures

"I had breakfast, lunch, and dinner with venture capitalists for two years prior to this, just getting their advice. They wanted a company that would be $50 million in revenue in five years. So I sat down in front of this Visi-Calc spreadsheet and I kept adding products until it added up to $50 million in five years."

$\mathcal{R}$obert (Bob) Metcalfe is a big, handsome, silver-haired guy who is a nest of contradictions. He looks—and acts—like a cross between a college basketball coach and a big-time corporate CEO. He is goofy and dignified, charming and spacey, urbane and yet sometimes shockingly innocent. He looks like a businessman but is pure nerd. And though he speaks of himself as a nonintellectual, Metcalfe is not only responsible for one of the biggest tech inventions of the last 20 years—the Ethernet, the heart of modern networking—but he also enunciated what is proving to be one of the greatest laws of the digital age.

Metcalfe and I first crossed paths almost two decades ago when I covered the story of 3Com for a tech magazine. Since then, he had left both the company and Silicon Valley, moving his family to the coast of Maine. A few years ago I assigned a feature writer to tell the story of Bob's new rural lifestyle. Like many of our readers, I found myself envying the world he had created for himself.

Just getting Metcalfe to California was tough. A deeply committed family man, he allows himself only a certain amount of travel each year, and once he has met that quota, it is hard to pry him out of Maine. I had bumped into him at a movie premiere on a previous trip. Obviously lonely for his kids, Bob had spent more time talking with my 10-year-old son than with the Valley leaders standing around him.

Finally, we were able to get Metcalfe to agree to a shoot, piggybacked on another business trip. He arrived at the studio his usual self: distracted, quizzical, and slightly amused by the idea of talking about himself. He was dressed in the usual all-over urban black that is his standard travel wear. As the interview progressed, his tiny grin grew, as if a national television interview was of such small potatoes to him at this point in his career that he could treat it as a cat's-paw, an intellectual puzzle to be probed and pushed and played with.

Throughout the interview, Metcalfe was astonishingly self-effacing: How many other entrepreneurs would admit to being a failure as a businessman? More impressive still, he seemed without much guile. As executive producer Bob Grove noted as Metcalfe trotted off, the man we'd seen that day in front of the cameras was identical to the one Grove had watched two weeks before, addressing the Rotary Club in Camden, Maine.

In the '80s, when I was selling the idea that Ethernet should be a standard, I had to explain why small networks were not being found to be valuable, but large networks were. So I made a slide that showed the value of the network growing linearly with the number of nodes and the value of the network growing as the square of the number of nodes, because each additional person not only could connect to everybody on the network, but added to the number of people that the others could connect to, and squared.

Now it's called Metcalfe's law. I'm grateful to George Gilder for calling it that. That's one of the rules about laws. You're not allowed to name them after yourself. You have to trick somebody else into doing it.

People take it more seriously than I do. For me it was a 35-millimeter slide that I used in presentations in the early '80s. It's not really a law—please. Moore's law has been true since 1965, and it's been exactly true. I don't think Metcalfe's law has ever been true in a numerical sense.

Accidental Engineer

I was born in 1946 in Brooklyn, and then moved slowly out onto Long Island. Most of my growing up was in Bayshore in the developments. We lived at 1048 South Thompson Drive, amidst single-story ranch brick houses, all of them identical.

My father was a technician and he never went to college. He started out as a technician and after 30 years he was an engineer. He was a test engineer on gyroscopic platforms for military platforms of various kinds, including missiles, at American Bosch Armor Corporation, an aerospace company in Garden City, New York.

When I was in seventh or eighth grade, the missiles started taking off successfully—Saturns and Atlases and all the rest—so he got a promotion, and we moved into the incorporated village inside of Bayshore, which is called Brightwaters. And there the houses were all different.

My father was an entrepreneur briefly. He started a company called BAM Electronics—Bailey, Abrahamson, and Metcalfe—repairing televisions. Mom was a Rosie-the-Riveter. She met my dad in Brooklyn during the war. Then she became a housewife. When we all went away to school, she became a secretary in the high school.

My grandmother, Nanny Bird, may she rest in peace, was tough. Norwegian tough. She worked with the Waterfront Commission of New York, which was created to fight organized crime.

Her job was to supervise the hiring of longshoremen by stevedores on the docks in New York, starting every morning at 5 A.M.

She would come out from Brooklyn to where we were living on Long Island, and she'd bring cheesecake every Friday night and spend the weekend with us. Then Monday morning she'd go out and deal with the dockworkers on the waterfront. What little tough I have, I got from her. [*Laughs.*]

My parents had two goals. One was to retire early, which they did, and the other one was to get me through college, and they succeeded in spades. I went to school for 23 years in a row.

I decided I wanted to go into electronics—into technology, really—early on, around fourth grade. I was writing a book report, and, typical of me, I did it the night before. I went down to the basement, where my father had a shop with some books on the shelf. I chose a book, and it turned out to be a college textbook in electrical engineering.

Well, I couldn't read it, but I wrote the book report. You know: "This book had its high points, and it had its low points, but overall it was an average book." This book happened to be written by MIT professors, two of them. So as a gratuitous comment, obviously calculated to brownnose my fourth-grade teacher, I wrote that I planned to go to MIT and get a degree in electrical engineering. Period. And I did just that. [*Laughs.*] Having written that sentence, I felt I had to do it.

We had electric trains set up in the basement on a sheet of painted green plywood. In the eighth grade, 1959, I built a computer. We used toggle switches and relays and neon lights. When it came time to build my little computer, I went down and, on a piece of paper, I figured out every possible combination of switch and light so that it would work.

It wasn't exactly a computer, but my science teacher called it one. It had six switches on it, so on the top bank you chose any number among 1, 2, and 3. On the bottom bank you chose another number among 1, 2, and 3, and then there were lights labeled 2, 3,

4, 5, and 6, and the correct light would light up, to show the sum of the two numbers.

Arpanetted

MIT was wonderful. I loved every minute of it. Solid-state electronics was emerging just about that time. We still had analog computers. I did take a transistor course, but tubes were still around.

I got into programming pretty early. My fraternity brothers said that if you wanted to make good money in the summer, you should take 6251, which was Systems Programming. And to take 6251 you had to take 645, which was Introduction to Programming. So I took those two courses, and by my sophomore year I was employed full-time, 12 months a year, all the way through college.

That was sick. And I played varsity sports—squash and tennis. I don't know when I slept.

I started out being a systems programmer, dealing with teletypes and communication devices sending characters to the teletype over the modem line. After I graduated from MIT, I went to Harvard graduate school for applied mathematics. That is where I ran into the Arpanet as a research project. I made it my graduate work. The Internet was allegedly born in September of '69, and I think I got involved in January of '70. That's how I really got into networking.

I joined Xerox PARC [Palo Alto Research Center, birthplace of the PC and Windows] in June of '72. There was a lot of great computer science done there in the late '70s and during the '80s. I joined the effort to try to commercialize, but it didn't work. I feel that whatever screwing up was done, I was part of it. So I don't try to blame it on others.

The Ethernet really came about on May 22, 1973. I was brought in as the networking guy since I had done my Ph.D. work on the Arpanet. The lab was building a minicomputer. So I was given the job of putting that minicomputer onto the Arpanet, which I had done at MIT. So I just did it again for Xerox Research.

*Scout's honor: The All-American Boy Genius
in appropriate garb.*

Then our next project was to build a bunch of personal computers. I got the job of putting those personal computers on the Arpanet and also connecting them to a laser printer, the first laser printer.

So, faced with that, using what I had learned from the Arpanet and the Aloha Network, on May 22, 1973, I wrote a memo sort of sketching the plan for Ethernet.

The modus operandi in Xerox PARC was that we built our own tools, our own toys, and there would be a computer on every desk. That was revolutionary in '72, '73. So I had to build a network that would connect hundreds of computers, separated by hundreds of meters, transmitting data at hundreds of kilobits per second, and out popped Ethernet.

It was a new problem. It was a problem no one else had. And it was great fun. They were the best years of my life because I had complete freedom to do any project I wanted. I had complete freedom and all the money in the world. I traveled first class, had assistants, capital equipment. It was heaven on earth.

I don't think there was a downside. [*Laughs.*] Oh, I'm sorry. There was a downside. I ended up getting divorced. I spent too much time at work, I think.

When I'm asked the question; What would you have done differently in your life?, the answer I have settled on is: I would have been a better salesman during 1979 and 1980 in convincing IBM to adopt Ethernet instead of running off and doing its Token Ring. I didn't sell well. I made it into a fencing contest. I believe I won the arguments. I just lost the sale.

Token Ring shipped in '85 or '86, which, history will record, is the beginning of the end for IBM as the standard setter in the industry.

Com, Com, Com

I left Xerox PARC because I got itchy. I have a short attention span, and I wanted to do something bigger and more interesting and more lucrative. I was frustrated at Xerox in that we had not figured out how to bring these products to market, and I wanted to bring products to market.

Xerox owned the rights to my Ethernet work. And so I just went and spent five or six months snooping around, trying to decide what kind of company to start.

I had started three little consulting companies when I was a student at MIT and Harvard. I had gone through the process of creating a company, having stationery printed, having business cards. And they lasted a year or two.

The new company's name was always 3Com. It was incorporated that way. Computer, communication, compatibility—com, com, com, 3Com.

Initially, 3Com was a consulting company—Digital Equipment Corporation, General Electric Company, and Exxon Corporation were our major clients. I was very comfortable with big companies because I'd worked at Xerox for eight years. I helped persuade DEC, Intel, and Xerox to get together to make Ethernet a standard. As soon as that had been accomplished, which was approximately May of '79, I said, "Aha! I should start a company to serve the Ethernet-compatible market that is sure to develop." The plan was, as soon as DEC, Intel, and Xerox published the specs for the Ethernet standard, then I would launch the big company.

I had two apartments. One in Boston, where I was hanging out for that five months of exploratory period. And then I had an apartment in Palo Alto at Oak Creek Apartments on Sand Hill Road—right next to the money guys. So I incorporated from Boston as a California company, and the first offices of 3Com were around my round orange dining room table at Oak Creek Apartments.

I had a business plan ready in September '80, when DEC, Intel, and Xerox published the specs. The specs were actionable. So I peddled this business plan. I didn't know anything about developing a long-term business plan for a manufacturing corporation. I made up the numbers. Spreadsheets were new.

They wanted five years of numbers. That didn't convince them. I was a pro, though, because they also noticed almost at once that my plan did not distinguish cash from profit. A bad start.

I went out and started assembling the resources to grow this company, and people, of course, are the most important resource, and I did a pretty good job. I started recruiting people who knew how to run companies much bigger than 3Com was, or was planning to be for a long time. And pretty quickly I built a company that I was incompetent to run, although I didn't realize it at the time.

I had built the board of directors very carefully. It was a first-rate board. I put a lot of time into that. And then, finally, the board said, "You know, Bill Krause should run the company because he knows how to do it and you don't." That was a horrible time for me.

It was devastating. But I had built this board. I had recruited these four or five or six people and the one job boards are supposed to do is choose the CEO. I was tempted to make a rather rude gesture and storm off and drive off into the night.

To show you how desperate we were, they made me head of sales and marketing. They said, "You know how to do that." I don't know why they thought I knew how to do that, but they made me head of sales and marketing, and so I had a job if I wanted one. So I was chairman of the board and head of sales, vice president of sales and marketing, starting June of '82. It was a credit to both Bill Krause and I that we did not kill each other but we came close many times.

I stayed at 3Com until 1990. The last two or three years, I realize in retrospect, the company had outgrown me again. It was clear, just looking at the numbers, that the company was stalled. It had grown to $400 million by that time and the numbers had flattened. We decided that the company was going sideways, it wasn't going forward. And the best thing to do was to get a fresh viewpoint. It was clear that Bill Krause and I had to go.

Eating My Words

I was finished at 3Com. In fact, I should have left several years earlier. I had sort of peaked out, and so I needed to do something different. I started writing. I liked the idea that I didn't have to supervise anyone. I could do it by myself all alone in my office, and it was dealing with ideas, and it was something to master.

I'm a bit different than most of the journalists I meet. I know about technology and business, and most of the journalists I meet don't know anything about either. They're English majors.

The other thing is, I'm a conservative, a Republican, a right-wing kook, you might say. And there are no journalists like that. Very few of them. So I thought I would help balance the journalistic profession by being a right-wing journalist.

Joining IDG *InfoWorld* was a way of staying in touch with this industry that I've grown up in and yet doing something completely different, something that doesn't require me to supervise large numbers of people, which is really hard work, especially if you want to do it well.

Over the last nine years, I've written 500 columns and I've made many predictions. I make a few big ones and occasionally I miss. I did miss one, unfortunately, where I promised to eat my column if I missed, and I ended up eating it in front of a large audience. Now I'm better known for having eaten my column than for having invented Ethernet. I like provoking people to tell me what an idiot I am.

It was a publicity stunt, basically. But I had to eat a lot of things in the corporate world, too [*chuckles*], usually in front of analysts every quarter.

I designed the 3Com logo: 3, capital C, small "om." I spent most of my time at 3Com being sure people spelled it exactly that way. No hyphens, no slashes. When I fly into San Francisco and I drive up to the city, I go by 3Com Park. It feels great, and I think the fact that they spell 3Com correctly is great.

After 3Com, I went to the University of Cambridge in England as a visiting fellow for a year. I've also moved to Maine for a bunch of reasons. It's the opposite of California. A change of scenery and it's close to MIT, where I'm quite active. My kids were pretty young then, and we were bothered by the opulence. We lived in Woodside, California, which is really wonderful, a gorgeous place. But the opulence of it disturbed me — we didn't know how to raise kids in it. Our kids are now in a small private school down the street.

People who find themselves in the situation I found myself in in 1990 frequently call me. "Well, you've been through this, you know, you've left your company," or "What did you do?" My advice usually is, "Take some time off. Don't jump into anything. You'll make a mistake. Relax. You deserve a vacation." But many make the mistake of jumping immediately into a new venture.

I think the motive [for rushing into another job] is that you get used to being important, and you can't stand not being important. So you take time off and you realize that, you know, you're relaxing, you have all the time in the world, but no one cares about you anymore, and you're not important, so you quickly have to replace that. You don't know what it's like not to be important. It's sort of like a rebound marriage. People who get into rebound marriages just can't imagine what it's like not to be married, so they get married again quickly, and they usually make a mistake.

I think entrepreneurs are different from each other. I see no pattern that I can apply. Maybe it's boredom. That is, the desire to avoid being bored, or a short attention span, or the need to make noise, or be noticed, or be important, or something, is what drives them. But beyond that, I don't see any pattern in them.

Looking back, I'd be reluctant to change anything. It's worked out so well for me . . . and I'm afraid that if I were to go back into the past and change one little thing, it would all unravel.

≋

A few months after the shoot, I contacted Metcalfe as part of a teleconference interview with him and Gordon Moore. The two men, responsible for the two defining laws of the Digital Age, barely knew each other. It was a little moment of history, and, as I understand it, the beginning of a growing friendship between the two men.

But what I remember most about that interview, which took place in December 1999, was a prediction. Both men were as confused as everyone else about the Internet bubble, and neither had any idea how long it would last. But when I asked Metcalfe when he thought it would burst, he jokingly predicted two weeks hence. Then, more seriously, he guessed March 2000. That proved to be, of course, the beginning of the first dot-com stock market crash. Bob Metcalfe, who once had to literally eat the words of his wrong prediction, this time called it right.

Photo by John Harding

Nolan Bushnell
Founder, Atari

The Man
- Born February 15, 1943
- Earned an engineering degree from the University of Utah
- Married, eight children

The Entrepreneur
- During the past 20 years, founded over 20 companies
- Founded Atari in 1972 with $250 at the age of 27, later sold it for $28 million
- Opened the first Chuck E. Cheese Pizza Time Theater in San Jose, California, in 1978
- Founded Uwink in 1999

"I used to say the difference between an entrepreneur and an employee is how you feel about payday. If you love them, you're an employee. If you hate them, you're an employer. And the number of times that it was Wednesday and payday was Friday and there was not enough money in the bank to make the payroll . . . it happened over and over and over again."

*W*hen I first met Nolan Bushnell, he was King of the Entre- preneurs. Five years before, he had created one of the great mira- cles of the electronics age. Working in the bedroom of a tiny house in Santa Clara, while his wife and two daughters slept, Bushnell had conceived a new product: a pinball-like arcade game designed to replicate the games he'd played on giant mainframe computers in college.

He tested his electronic Ping-Pong game at Andy Capp's pub on El Camino in Sunnyvale one June evening in 1972. As the leg- end goes, the owner of the bar angrily called to complain that the machine had already broken down after a few hours . . . only to have Bushnell's coworker discover that the machine was jammed with the quarters of obsessed players. Bushnell realized he had a hit on his hands.

And a company as well: Atari, the first great skyrocketing, high- living, countercultural start-up. Atari was the prototype of all that followed, from Apple Computer to the legion of dot-coms. But none matched the original. Atari was long-haired freaks and slick salespeople, hot tub parties and products code-named after the sexiest women employees. And presiding over it all, the ego and the id of high tech, the tallest man in any room, with custom suits and a head full of curls, was Nolan Bushnell.

For a time, he was the most famous businessman in America. He ran Atari right to the top, until it became synonymous with the digital revolution itself—then quit. He sold the company in 1976 to Warner Communications for $28 million and took off on new adventures.

It was during this period that I first met Bushnell. He was still elegantly dressed and coiffed, but he met me in an old Sunnyvale warehouse. There, with typically overwhelming enthusiasm, he showed me a weird collection of giant robot dolls. This, he told me, puffing on his pipe, is the heart of my new business: pizza parlors!

It seemed a crazy idea. But Bushnell's eye for new business opportunities was unequaled. Pizza Time Theaters made him a second fortune.

In the years that followed, I visited with Bushnell several times. At our last meeting he sat in his office at his new business incubator, Catalyst, and described how he was going to turn the room into a worldwide command center where, like some kind of wired mastermind—a Dr. Mabuse of consumer tech—he would control the operations of a dozen or more new companies at the same time. After all he had accomplished, who could doubt that Bushnell would conquer this, too?

But Catalyst collapsed in bankruptcies, lawsuits, and recriminations. And Nolan Bushnell faded away. For a while, he was reportedly working out of San Francisco and acting as an angel investor. But, while working on a book about Apple Computer (Bushnell had "discovered" Steve Jobs), I tried to contact Bushnell's office. He was gone.

We were preparing *Betting It All*, scheduling our entrepreneurs, when I happened upon a copy of the San Jose alternative weekly, *Metro*. There, on the cover, was Nolan, his hair now gray and short, but with the old gleam in his eye. He had been found by a young reporter.

The story *Metro* told was a poignant one: The King of the Entrepreneurs had lost everything in lawsuits brought by Merrill Lynch, and was now living with his family in a small rented house in southern California. After some searching, we found him and flew him to San Jose for the shoot.

I was afraid it would be a painful reunion. After all, Bushnell knew I would be probing not only his successes, but also the causes of his fall.

Instead, I found the Nolan Bushnell I once knew. Funny, charismatic, larger than life, and forever optimistic about his next big project. After 20 years, little had changed. I again found myself happy to be in his company, listening to his dreams, laughing at his jokes. For an instant, Silicon Valley was young again, and Nolan Bushnell was ready to take on the world and win.

The Catalyst

The catalyst for developing a video game was seeing a low price on a minicomputer for about $3,000. All of a sudden, I said, "That would work in an amusement park."

My plan was to create an interface to a regular television set. In those days, the display systems were $6,000 each. So I thought my innovation would be to take the minicomputer and interface it to a regular television set. I was going to run six screens off of one mini-computer, and put it in an amusement park, and then I could amortize the costs of the big, expensive minicomputer over six coin slots.

There was a guy who did a minicomputer game and had it in the Stanford Copy Center. I moved my daughter out of her bedroom and made it into my lab. I never did build the minicomputer base system. I kept running out of cycle time, so I had to keep making the terminals smarter. Finally I said, "Hey, I'm just going to throw this away and make the terminal totally smart," and then the economics worked really well. Much better than anticipated.

I had dinner with my daughter last night and we were talking about this. She said, "The nice thing about being the daughter who gave up the bedroom is that I always get mentioned in the articles." Her name is Britta.

Al Alcorn worked for me at Ampex. It was actually Al who built the first Pong machines. I put Pong in a bar in Sunnyvale called Andy Capp's and offered to share the revenue. I got a call later on that night that the Pong machine wasn't working any more. The tavern owner is on the phone saying, "Hey, look, you put this thing in here today. It's already busted. Get over here and get it fixed."

So Al goes over, and he pulls the coin box out. The quarters were backed up through the coin slot. It had earned so much money that the coin box was too small and was jammed. That's the kind of problem I can solve. In the coin-operated game business, the coin box never lies to you.

Just that day, I had told Al, "If this game earns $10 a day, we've got a hit." It earned $40 a day. So it was almost an order of magnitude, and I was thinking, "I've got to build these things as fast as humanly possible."

We looked at 100 percent of the resources we had in terms of all the money we could beg, borrow, and steal, and the answer came up that we could buy the parts for 11 units. And so that was our first run. We made a production run of 11 units.

I tried to get venture capital money, to no avail. What people don't understand is that innovation is the hardest thing in the world to fund. We had a lot of problems. First of all, in those days, the coin-operated game business was considered to be controlled by the Mafia.

Second, it was a game. It wasn't building steel or cars or disk drives or strong computers that were going to do accounting things. This was a game. And whether we like it or not, we are a Calvinistic society in which we consider things to do with entertainment somewhat trivial and a little bit sinful. So this was very difficult. The reason that I raised no venture capital until we were $40 million in sales wasn't because I didn't want to. It was because I couldn't. I was also 28 years old, and this was before it was good to be a 28-year-old entrepreneur.

But I was able to ramp pretty fast. We were able to end that six months at over $4 million in sales. The following year, we made $11 million, and the year after that, we made $23 million, all on internally generated funds.

We went to the New York toy fair with a consumer version of Pong. We put it on the table, and had a booth, the whole thing. We sold none. Zero.

At that time, toy stores said, "$29 is the most expensive toy I have," and all of a sudden, I was asking for $99. They said, "Can't do it." So we went to appliance stores, where they sell television sets. A natural. "Well, we don't think so. People will want to finance it. It's $100 and if they get tired of it before the payments are out, we might have a problem."

So we tried the Magnavox stores. We tried the GE stores. We tried the department stores with their brown goods, as they're called. And no takers.

And then we called the guy who's running the sporting goods department at Sears. Unbeknownst to us, his mainstay in the winter months was selling pool tables and Ping-Pong tables. He thought to himself a year earlier that, "Gee, pool tables are in bars, and I'm selling a lot of pool tables for garage and rumpus rooms. Maybe a pinball machine." So he marketed a small pinball machine for the home, and did very well.

He visited us, saw the game, and said, "Okay, how many can you build?" We thought we could build about 25,000. Everyone warned us that we didn't want to do an exclusive deal with Sears, because if they went away, then all of a sudden, the business goes.

He came back the following day with a purchase order for 150,000. I started going through the numbers and realized that there was no way we could finance it. So I called him and said, "Tom, I'm sorry. We can't finance this." And he said, "Oh, no problem. Let me introduce you to Sears Bank."

What they did was set up an accounts-receivable facility that essentially bought units when they dropped off the end of our production line. They went into the cage, because they wanted them all delivered in September, October, which says that we had to build them most of the year. And so basically we got advanced 80 percent of our sales price as they dropped off the end. And that made the numbers work.

Baptism by Fire

I started working with my dad when I was nine. My dad owned a construction company in Utah. It wasn't a huge company, but it was a nice little family business. He was severely dyslexic and could not read as an adult, though he was a very successful businessman. He took me to work with him to read for him. I was his scribe.

My mother did all the books for the company and that sort of thing. She did the contracts and he'd negotiate them. He was a great manager and was able to always figure out the right economics.

I was a ham radio operator when I was 11. I think I was one of the youngest ones in Utah.

But if you take your allowance and what you can earn mowing lawns and divide it into a $400 radio or a transmitter that you want to buy, the math doesn't work. So I said, "How am I going to earn more money?" I answered my own question by setting up a TV and appliance repair business part-time.

In those days, the TV set was really an icon in the living room. To let an 11-year-old kid come in and mess with it took a certain leap of faith. What I did was offer to do a service call for 50 cents. A service call in those days was usually $5 to $10 so I really priced myself into the market. They thought, "Well, we'll really take advantage of this kid."

The word got around that I could actually fix the things. What they didn't realize was that I really marked up the tubes that I replaced. It's what I call "stealth marketing." I charged 50 cents in the door, and all of a sudden, the tubes were pretty expensive. I did very well.

Then my father died when I was 16. My father's death was a turning point in my life. I'm from a very traditional Mormon family and in the Mormon world the male is the head of the household. It's not very politically correct these days. But with the passing of my father, I had a mother and three sisters; I was expected to shoulder the burden. It wasn't even a question. It wasn't like somebody said, "Now, Nolan, you do it." I just knew what I had to do and I did it.

I ran the construction team as a 16-year-old until school started that year, when I actually closed his business down. That was what we call "baptism by fire," in terms of the entrepreneurial stuff.

On the Midway

I went to Utah State to start, but I graduated from the University of Utah. I decided that I wanted to be an entrepreneur. There was an amusement park two towns up, which is not very far away in Utah. A lot of my associates, the guys I went to high school with, worked at that amusement park. But I always thought that you couldn't make enough money at it. So I started a business called the Campus Company, which was basically a throwaway advertising company.

Basically I took a blotter-sized piece of paper, set up advertising all around it, and put a calendar of events in the middle. The idea was that you would sell $6,000 worth of advertisements, print it up for $500, then give them away free at the beginning of the school year. And you pocket the rest. I did that for several universities.

It was a time when no matter how much money you had, it wasn't quite enough. I felt that, in order to really do it up right, I

Sideshow: Away from the carnival midway, Nolan Bushnell was a serious young engineer.

needed to protect myself from myself—because if I had money and I had time, I would spend it.

So I thought, "I'll get a part-time job working nights at the amusement park. It'll be fun. And it'll keep me out of financial harm's way." I found that I actually had a kind of an affinity for it. What I hadn't realized is that, yeah, they had a low hourly salary, but they also had a commission on sales.

My earliest job at the amusement park was running the Midway. It put me in contact with literally thousands of people a day. I began to see how people work. I did it as a part-time job, just summers.

I worked the "one ball," where you throw one ball and see if you can knock the bottles down. If you do, you win a stuffed animal. I also did guessing ages, weights, and occupations.

There used to be a dance hall close by and people would bring dates down. It was always so fun because generally there'd be four or five couples standing around. I would try to pick out which one of those guys was considered the epsilon male—the one who has the girlfriend that isn't the cheerleader, and who's sort of the hanger-on to the group. He wins the stuffed animal. Then the alpha male spends all the money he has trying to do the same.

So here I was, a college kid at 20 years old, running a $3 million operation with 150 employees. And this was just the Midway section. I didn't run the rides and the food operations, but it was still a big responsibility.

In the spring quarter when the park was open, my grades suffered. I was studying engineering and technology. What was very interesting to me, though, was a guy named Dr. Evans, of Evans & Sutherland fame. He was attaching video screens to a big digital computer, which was new. In the middle '60s, the only places that had video screens on computers were Stanford, the University of Utah, MIT, and the University of Minnesota, I think.

All of a sudden, on that screen I saw a game that was written by a student at MIT called "Space War." It changed my life. So when people say, "Are you the father of video game?" I have to say, "No,

I really saw one at the University of Utah, and thought to myself, "I want that at my amusement park."

But I knew I couldn't do it. The economics weren't right. I divided 25 cents per play into the $7 million it costs for the machine and the math didn't work. So I just sort of filed the idea away in the back of my mind.

Hitting the Road

When I graduated from college, I actually had two career paths. Since I had the highest per capita game revenue of any amusement park in the country, I had all kinds of offers coming in to run other amusement parks. And I always felt that I could do that at any time.

But I also had this fresh engineering degree. I was interested in technology, and I said, "Let me just see what this is like. I've worked in amusement parks. I know what that's all about. Let's go the technology road."

I really liked a lot of things about Utah. But I always felt that I was destined to be a player on a different stage. I was married to my college sweetheart. We met at a fraternity/sorority rush and had a child. We pointed the car west, came to California, and I got a job at Ampex.

I remember telling my wife, as we came down off the mountains and through Sacramento. "I'll have my own company in two years." And, of course, my wife said, "Oh, yes, Nolan." You know.

As a company, Ampex was completely off the wall. But more than that, the company had a very, very good atmosphere for creative outlets. I learned a huge amount at Ampex. I would say that was my technical underpinning, more than my college days. I had a couple of great mentors there from the technical side.

Ampex had its problems, though. Some companies are technologically driven. They may have some foibles in marketing or some other things, but their brilliance sustains them through that.

But if you snuff that brilliance out and become expense focused as opposed to sales focused, the innovation stops. The company fails.

Pacmanship

I am a technologist. I have a degree in engineering. But I also have a degree in business, and I do all my own spreadsheets and financial planning. If people were to ask me, what was the hardest thing to do at Atari, I tell them, it was running the company without money. The company started with $250 and went to $40 million in sales without a penny of venture capital.

I feel like I'm best at creating the path through the jungle with a machete, never necessarily traveling that path again. And I like to make sure that the economics are right. A lot of people don't understand that being a good entrepreneur has actually more to do with numbers than it does with concepts. Nobody thinks of me as a numbers guy, and that's always been an interesting disconnect with me.

I believe that you can be a great entrepreneur anytime. The real key is having judgment. You really need to make sure your numbers are right in the final analysis. Even though today with— I'll call it the Internet craziness—where people think that numbers don't matter, they will. Numbers always win finally. And you either have them or you don't.

The corporate culture at Atari was the biggest disconnect to the way business was run at that point in time. I would never allow anybody to have reserved parking spots. I thought the spots close to the building were reserved for those people who got there first. We really did have an egalitarian structure. Atari was really the genesis of dress-down Fridays.

We had a good time. I would set very aggressive goals for the company, and the reward for achieving them would be that there'd be a big party. I felt that Atari really fine-tuned the carrot approach to management as opposed to the stick. We said, "This is an outrageous goal. People are going to be working nights and weekends, but the reward is going to be outrageous fun." Besides it was the '70s, and it worked. It worked wonderfully. Everybody loved it. Everybody worked really, really hard.

Wired magazine did this terrific story that I was so proud of. They did a genealogy of Atari and of all its people. They followed the people after they left Atari. We were the genesis of over 200 companies in Silicon Valley.

W u n d e r k i n d

When I hired Steve Jobs, he wasn't Steve Jobs. He was this odd guy who nobody really understood and wasn't especially liked. But he was brilliant. I felt, and still do, that if you create 100 percent meritocracy, and you are an astute manager, then you should be able to deal with all other issues that come up.

I had groups of engineers off in side buildings just so they could bring their dog in and have a six-pack of beer in the refrigerator—which wasn't appropriate for the mainline company. Other people worked nights just because everybody hated them. You know, the whole personality issue.

Many times, truly brilliant people do not abide fools gladly. And they perceive anyone who is not as smart as they are as a fool. So should you fire that person just because he or she happens to have bad hygiene and bad manners?

I m p l o s i o n

Why did I sell and leave Atari? You know, I've asked myself that a hundred times, and I think it was because I was tired. *[Laughs.]* When you're running a company, it's your baby. You tend to not take a lot of time for yourself. My first marriage had dissolved, as many entrepreneurial marriages do, because of the job.

I was starting to date my current wife, Nancy, who's been one of the best things that's ever happened to me. But I didn't have any time. I didn't feel like I could really take the time. And more than that, I had a lot of ambition. But all of a sudden I was offered a lot of money. Companies rise, companies fall, but cash is cash. Twenty-eight million dollars, was one of the bigger buyouts of that time. It was a lot of money.

After I left Atari, it imploded. The reason Atari had been a rocket ship was that it had a whole series of things that were pushing the envelope. We would take pockets of talent, move them into slightly different areas so they could keep growing, creating a composite geometric curve of things that were going on. I stayed on at Atari for two years after I sold it, but it became very clear to me that the new owners had no interest in those innovative strategies.

I think that the major implosion was an embarrassment to Warner Communications. Remember: By this time, there were a lot of people who knew how to turn the crank of something that was already created, but they didn't know how to create. They didn't know how to *build*. If you look at the Atari implosion really as a time for rebuilding, the creative skill set wasn't there.

When Atari went, Japan took over. Nintendo, Sony—they still own the game business. That's in some ways maybe the greatest or the worst legacy of Atari. Name me one other time in which the market leader ever abandoned its market. It never happened.

When I sold Atari, I had a noncompete agreement in the video-game business, so I had to do something that would fit around my contractual obligation. I was too young to retire.

I had always felt that games were not presented to young children properly. The bowling alley isn't a good place for an eight-year-old. I also had this feeling that there were too many forces in society pulling families apart. I mean, what could you do with your eight-year-old? There was nothing.

Arcades are the purview or the hangout for teenagers. Eight-year-olds and teenagers don't mix. So I felt that I needed to have a nice game center, and pizza was part of the life support system for the game center.

In Chuck E. Cheese, I wanted to have the animals so that the parents would have something to do while the kids were in the game room. I knew that the kids would watch the animals for about three or four nanoseconds and then they'd be off into the game room. It was very successful.

I then started a whole bunch of companies. I was spending almost no time at Pizza Time, even though I was still chairman. I got very cocky. More than that, you have to pay attention. Because it had been easy, because it had been effortless, I put too much on my plate.

One of the things that you forget—and it's so easy to forget when you're riding so high—is how hard it is and how much effort each start-up takes. You forget the people. My dad would always say that the minute you think that the sun is shining out of your rear, all you have is an illuminated landing area.

By the time Pizza Time went through its problems, most people didn't realize I had resigned as chairman a year before. Some people still associated the troubles and failures with me. Even when you're not there, you're still there because your name is associated with it. If it goes down in flames, you're just gonna take one more hit to your reputation—when, in fact, you didn't really have your hands on the controls. It's like being charged as a drunk driver when you're a passenger.

The High Road

We went through 15 years of litigation. I think that my wife and I and my family grew very close during that period. It was a very, very good time for our family. I'm not sure that had not the adversity come in, we would have ended up being as neat a family as we've turned out to be.

I think, personally, it was also excellent for me. I mean, I was way too high. I don't think I would have been a good husband. And I did a very obvious and I did a purposeful thing, keeping quiet about it. I just feel like you shouldn't necessarily advertise certain problems.

If you decide you're gonna take the high road, you have to have a thick skin. You just have to deal with it and say, "I'm not going to believe that I'm a wonderful guy or a schmuck because they say that I am. I know who I am, and I'm gonna be a good family man and I'm going to take care of my kids and my wife and my wife's gonna take care of me and we're gonna have a great time. And we're gonna move forward. We're gonna make the future happen a little bit faster and that's what's fun."

≋

A few months after this interview, we held a party at *Forbes* magazine's West Coast Gallery to celebrate the completion of the edited series. We invited the guests of the series and, for fun, even rented a bunch of arcade games to line the hall. Bushnell arrived early and, as always, towered over the crowd.

After some small talk, Nolan Bushnell found himself invited over to play a game of Pong. He stayed there most of the evening. After a while, it was my turn to join him at the controls. I had waited much of my life for just this chance.

As the game began, as the little ball ricocheted around the screen, I happened to glance over at Bushnell. He was grinning, his face glowing with the thrill of competition. It was as if he was playing the game for the first time.

ABOUT THE AUTHOR

Michael S. Malone has been called "the Boswell of Silicon Valley" by the *San Jose Mercury News*. He was raised in Silicon Valley and holds a bachelor's degree in combined sciences and an M.B.A. from Santa Clara University. He hosted *Malone*, a half-hour interview program that ran for nine seasons and was seen on PBS stations nationwide. His current 16-part TV series, *Betting It All: The Entrepreneurs*, an in-depth look at some of America's most famous entrepreneurs, appeared on PBS stations beginning May 3, 2001.

Beyond the television programs, Malone is best known as an author. His first book, *The Big Score: The Billion Dollar Story of Silicon Valley* (Doubleday), was named one of the top 10 business books of 1985 by *Business Week*.

The book grew out of Malone's years at the *San Jose Mercury News* as the nation's first daily high-tech reporter, where he coauthored the first investigative stories on toxic waste contamination, workplace drug abuse, and sweatshops in Silicon Valley. *The Big Score* went on to become the basis for the KTEH documentary series *Silicon Valley*, which aired on PBS in 1987. Another documentary hosted and written by Malone, *Future Tense*, earned a 1996 cable television Telly award.

In the past decade, Malone's articles and editorials have appeared in such publications as the *New York Times* (where he was a columnist for two years), the *Wall Street Journal*, the *Economist*, *Forbes ASAP*, and *Fortune*. He was featured as a lead essayist (with Tom Wolfe and Mark Helprin) in the celebrated *Forbes ASAP* Big Issue (1996).

About his book, *Going Public* (HarperCollins), published in 1991, *Inc.* magazine wrote that it "contains all the suspense and intrigue of a Robert Ludlum thriller." In 1992, Malone coauthored (with William H. Davidow) *The Virtual Corporation* (Harper-

Collins), which became the subject of a cover story in *Business Week* and was one of the most influential business books of the decade. *The Microprocessor: A Biography* (Telos/Springer-Verlag) was published in September 1995 and was the winner of a Critic's Choice award. *Virtual Selling* (Free Press), coauthored with Tom Siebel, was published in February 1996. *Intellectual Capital*, coauthored with Leif Edvinsson, was published by HarperBusiness in March 1997. His latest nonfiction book, *Infinite Loop: How the World's Most Insanely Great Computer Company Went Insane*, about Apple Computer, was published by Doubleday in February 1999. It was named one of the top tech and business books in 1999 by the *Library Journal.*

In August 1998, Malone was named editor of *Forbes ASAP.* He also has a weekly column on ABCNews.com called "Silicon Insider."

INDEX